Humanisation?

Unquenched desire, the dividing up of the drives, repetition, and symptom are the keywords for the effects that the unconscious, as deciphered by Freud, has on the body. Harmony is not on the agenda, but rather the discordance, unlinking, and arrogance of cynical jouissances. It seems that the discourse of capitalism is today increasing their deleterious consequences – with all of these demonstrative suicides, but also suicides as diverse as those of terrorists, Tibetan monks, those beleaguered by the capitalist enterprise, and all the hopeless of our time. Hence the question that Lacan posed concerning the possible "humanisation" of this denatured animal, about whom Freud did not hesitate to say that he is a wolf to man, even though he has always made community. What will the psychoanalyst say about possible solutions, he whose act excludes the call to norms of any kind?

Humanisation? is the 2013–2014 volume of the annual seminar held by Colette Soler at the Clinical College of the Lacanian Field in Paris.

Colette Soler practices and teaches psychoanalysis in Paris. She holds an agrégation in philosophy and a doctorate in psychology. It was her encounter with the teaching and person of Jacques Lacan that led her to choose psychoanalysis. She was a member of the École Freudienne de Paris and, following its dissolution, became the Director of the École de la Cause Freudienne, after which she was at the forefront of the movement of the International of the Forums and its School of Psychoanalysis.

Humanisation?

Psychoanalysis, Symbolisation, and the Body of the Unconscious

Colette Soler

Translated by Benjamin Farrow and Hugues d'Alascio

LONDON AND NEW YORK

First published 2018
by Routledge
2 Park Square, Milton Park, Abingdon, Oxon OX14 4RN

and by Routledge
711 Third Avenue, New York, NY 10017

Routledge is an imprint of the Taylor & Francis Group, an informa business

© 2018 Colette Soler

The right of Colette Soler to be identified as author of this work has been asserted by her in accordance with sections 77 and 78 of the Copyright, Designs and Patents Act 1988.

All rights reserved. No part of this book may be reprinted or reproduced or utilised in any form or by any electronic, mechanical, or other means, now known or hereafter invented, including photocopying and recording, or in any information storage or retrieval system, without permission in writing from the publishers.

Trademark notice: Product or corporate names may be trademarks or registered trademarks, and are used only for identification and explanation without intent to infringe.

British Library Cataloguing-in-Publication Data
A catalogue record for this book is available from the British Library

Library of Congress Cataloging-in-Publication Data
A catalog record has been requested for this book

ISBN: 978-1-78220-623-1 (pbk)

Typeset in Times New Roman
by Apex CoVantage, LLC

Contents

Foreword   viii

I   13th November 2013   1
The name man   1
Without the Other   4
The inhuman unconscious   7

II   27th November 2013   10
The denatured   10
Real effects of the symbolic   11
Effects on the real   14

III   11th December 2013   19
Jouissance, fitted out   19
   Motérialité   20
   Object a, the orphan   23
   Destructivity?   26

IV   25th January 2014   27
Tragedy or destructivity?   27
L'(a)cause première   29
New problems   30
The agalma of desire   31

V   29th January 2014   34
Types of desires   35
What does the analyst want?   36
Up to what point does logic command?   40

VI 12th February 2014   44

The highway of the metaphor 46
The paternal order 48
The name of the Thing 51

VII 5th March 2014   53

Diagnoses according to the metaphor 53
The names of the name 54
Function of the exception 56
The saying as exception 58

VIII 19th March 2014   61

No discourse of *suppléance* 62
Before, after 63
The function (Φx) 65
   Phallic signification 65
   The jouissance of the phallus 67

IX 2nd April 2014   69

Speech as cause 69
The propositional function 73
Ex-sistence 74

X 7th May 2014   77

Two halves? 77
Various not-alls 80
   The not-all of psychosis 80
   The not-all of women 83
   A not-all society? 84

XI 21st May 2014   87

A father 87
The father of the name 88
   The function of the name 89
   The function of naming 91

XII 4th June 2014 **95**
    Name and naming 95
    A new father 97
    Not without the father 99
    But fatherless 100

References   104
Index   107

Foreword

Colette Soler has been practicing and teaching psychoanalysis in Paris and in various regions of the world for many years. Several of her works are already known to the English-speaking world.[1] Since 1998, she has held a seminar at the Clinical College of the Lacanian Field in Paris. The texts that have issued from her teaching have been in circulation for some time now and have inspired study and research within the psychoanalytic community across the globe, spanning diverse linguistic zones.

We now come to the present publication of the 2013–2014 seminar: *Humanisation?*, published in French in Paris in 2014 and then in Italian in Rome in 2016. It figures among other interesting titles such as: *La querelle des diagnostics, Avènements du réel: de l'angoisse au symptôme, Qu'est-ce que l'inconscient?, Ce qui reste de l'enfance, Vers l'identité, Qu'est-ce qui fait lien?,* and many others. It now appears in English thanks to the work of our colleagues from the Forums of the Lacanian Field of Paris and London: Benjamin Farrow and Hugues d'Alascio, who undertook the work of translation, and Daphne and Nestor Tamarin who recognised the enthusiasm that this work had generated among seminar participants and contributed to the realisation of this publication.

This teaching requires the reader to pull his own weight because it tends to question Lacan's theses and to elaborate on them. Working with the theme, "The unconscious and the body", Colette Soler situates her remarks within the problems of our time, starting with all of the reworkings of the family, with questions regarding filiation, modes of reproduction, figures of sexuality, and everything that the symbolic before science used to put into order through the master's discourse. We are thus able to recognise what is specific to the Lacanian field, as Lacan called it, in treating the question of the humanisation of desire.

Freud rooted his theory in the myths and classical figures of the family. Lacan returned to Freud and went beyond Oedipus[2] to renew the psychoanalytic clinic. In reformulating the paternal function beyond the oedipal myth, he extended the function of metaphorisation to that of naming. Colette Soler pursues the question regarding what can produce a truly human formation by considering the structural brake that accompanies language itself. A human formation passes through language, which has real effects on the real of what is living and which puts the brakes on jouissance.

Humanisation? The term carries with it all of the ambiguities that are attached to the name … man, with all of the corresponding idealisations. Every colonisation was carried out in the name of a supposed humanisation. Following Lacan, who, inventing a neologism, spoke of "the prevailing humanitarianery in which our abuses cloak themselves" (1974, p. 54), Colette Soler goes on to ask "under what conditions the humanisation of the child can be anything other than the colonising humanitarianery of the underdeveloped". The term humanisation indicates the necessity of a "grafting of culture for the little premature one who is the child of man", and the question mark interrogates its current forms. How can a speech that names be grafted? How is a proper name invented? She questions the current conditions of "our worry about a human formation". Lacan said that, "every human formation has as its essence, and not by accident, the curbing of jouissance" (Lacan, 1967), namely the bending of the body to the most basic demands of social life.

Colette Soler has already worked on the steps that led Lacan to "assert an unprecedented formula, the formula that says against all expectation that the unconscious – until then always described as symbolic – is real" (Soler, 2014, p. xv). She uses the term RUCS in order to designate this real unconscious, which affects the body and its jouissance. Taking this development into account in psychoanalysis entails certain clinical, theoretical, and political consequences. The real that is proper to the unconscious is redoubled by the real that is proper to capitalism, which undoes traditional social links. Hence, the question: if we must give up oedipal identifications, "What is it then that will be able to humanise if not the real unconscious, or at least the no less real effects of it on those who speak?"

These remarks stand as an invitation to read this book in the hope that the reader, each in his own way, might proceed at his own pace.

Diego Mautino
Rome, December 3rd 2017

Notes

1 Soler, C. (2006). *What Lacan Said About Women: A Psychoanalytic Study*. J. Holland (Trans.). New York: Other Press; (2005). *The Era of Traumatism*. S. Roizin and B. Glaubach (Trans.). Rome: Biblink; (2014). *Lacan: The Unconscious Reinvented*. E. Faye and S. Schwartz (Trans.). London: Karnac; (2016). *Lacanian Affects: The Function of Affect in Lacan's Work*. B. Fink (Trans). New York: Routledge.
2 Oedipal ideology and "the specific attachment of the analyst to the coordinates of the family, […] is linked to a mode of questioning sexuality that seriously risks missing a sexual conversion that is taking place before our eyes" (Lacan, 2001d, p. 587).

Chapter 1

13th November 2013

My topic for this year is at the crossroads of several preoccupations that concern at once the trajectory of Lacan's teaching, the problems posed by the era that is ours, and the theme of the clinical colleges of the Lacanian field this year: "The unconscious and the body." The context of the era is made up of the reworkings of the family, with problems of filiation, of the modes of reproduction – in short, everything that the symbolic before science used to put into order. For this first lesson, I am going to indicate the axes of my question and thus announce the developments to come.

I said humanisation with a question mark. There is no doubt that a grafting of culture is necessary for the little premature one who is the child of man. It is not a question of assuring only his organic survival but of enabling him to be socialised. The case of so-called wild children, which today is no longer very current, made it possible, in the past, to grasp this frontier between survival and socialisation. But why call this process *humanisation*?

The term can be justified, we will see, but it is suspect because it carries with it all of the ambiguities which are attached to the name [*nom*] ... man with all of the corresponding idealisations. Remember the famous phrase from Maxim Gorki: "Man! It's magnificent. It sounds so noble!" Did he not think of himself as the pinnacle of creation, the one which Freud thinks he topples with his supposed Copernican revolution? As for Lacan, in order to sweep away this man [*homme*] seen from the locus of the Other, he resorts to phonetic writing: L.O.M., in order to connote only what is most real of it.

The name man

Indeed, as soon as we speak of socialisation, or of acculturation or of humanisation, we mobilise value judgements. It was very clear during the eras when one still used to speak of barbarians or of savages, thereby excluding them from civilised humanity, whom we identified with the particularities of a culture and specifically of a religion. All of the colonisations of the past, with the abuses that characterised them – to say the least – were carried out in the name of a supposed humanisation. Lacan has a beautiful expression, a very condensed one. He says: "The prevailing humanitarianery in which our abuses cloak themselves" (Lacan, 1974, p. 54).[1] The neological expression is interesting: it is constructed, like this other one from Lacan, linguistery, constructed in order to distinguish the use that psychoanalysis makes of language from that of linguistics as a discipline. This difference, Lacan says, is that psychoanalysis is less concerned with language as an object than with what has an effect within language. In the same way, what has an effect in the humanitarianery of colonisation are the expected surplus values. This is no longer a secret to anyone. We are certainly no longer in the time when the humanitarianery of the colonising mission was advanced under cover of religious conversion. The forms have changed with the development of capitalism, even to the point where the notion of colonisation is disappearing and being converted into economic imperialism, but the thesis remains the same: an obligation to mask the true motivation of companies with so-called human values. If you wish to recall another context for the same question, watch the movie *La Controverse de Valladolid*, a film made in 1992 by Jean-Daniel Verhaeghe, with Jean-Louis Trintignant, Jean-Pierre Marielle, and Jean Carmet. It is a very delightful, funny film that recreates something from this distant era, although it is not an accurate historical document. In the film, the question that is debated is one of knowing if Indians have a soul. In the real controversy, which was carried out according to the wishes of Charles V and which opposed the Dominican Bartolomé de Las Casas and the theologian Juan Ginés de Sepúlveda, in 1550 and 1551, it was a question of the forms that conquest should take, a conquest which had been suspended by Charles V following multiple criticisms during the entire first half of the sixteenth century of the crimes committed. It was not a question of denying their soul since they wanted to convert them. In short, one can wonder under what conditions the humanisation of the child can be anything other than the colonising humanitarianery of the underdeveloped. This is a first question.

So, I chose as a point of departure this term humanisation that Lacan used on several occasions, at least until 1969. And not to suggest that man, overtaken by modernity, would have entered into the civilisation of the inhuman [*inhumain*], far from it, because man, what we name "man", has in essence, the essence of language, always been surpassed by transcendent factors – the cause of his anxiety [*angoisse*] – whether they bear the names of the Greek gods, or of the gods of the monotheisms, or of that extimate transcendence that is the unconscious, or even ... the real. There is nothing that is not proper to man in this, so nothing inhuman [*inhumain*], unless one uses the terms humane [*humain*] and inhumane [*inhumain*], as values.[2]

During the *Journées* on the subject of psychosis and children of October 22nd 1967, Lacan evoked what he designated as "our worry about a human formation". He also talked about the "humanisation of desire". Would this imply that the desire of man, the substantive, is in itself rather ... inhuman, the adjective? But then the inhuman would be that which is proper to man.

In fact, the term appears to be dated. Indeed, it dates from an era – and Lacan mentions it – where one could think that the great structuralist moment, eminently represented by Lévi-Strauss with his *Elementary Structures of Kinship*, was announcing "the end of man", he who was previously thought as being endowed with free will, and who from then on was reduced to only being thought as the product of structures. I say man, but it was very specifically women, whether they like it or not, who within structure had come to occupy the role of objects of exchange. Who would dare to say this today? In 1967, in the speech to which I am referring, Lacan explicitly disagrees with this structuralist moment. I am quoting him, he is addressing psychoanalysts: "It does indeed seem that we risk forgetting in the field of our function that an ethic is in its principle [*est à son principe*] and that from now on, whatever may be said – and just as well without my avowal – about the end of man concerns a formation that we can qualify as human, which is our principal torment" (Lacan, 1967).

"Without my avowal": it's very clear, Lacan in no way validates the supposed end of man introduced by structuralism, nor that of woman. What follows proves it. This reference to ethics, that of psychoanalysis, excludes, in fact, that the one who speaks be only a marionette of that which transcends him, this, for us, being language and discourse. Lacan reaffirms here what he laid out beginning with his first works on psychosis: man is not man without freedom and the possible choices that it implies, madness included. Another question emerges then, which comes from around the same period. Would psychoanalysis be a humanism? This is what Sartre says about existentialism: "Existentialism is a humanism", a text from 1945, published in 1946, at the very end of the war. Here, we grasp that this word designates a value. In this formulation from Sartre, we perceive the nuance of defence against an accusation, that of attacking the essence of man, man with a capital M, with his thesis that posed that man is not a given, a nature, but that he forges himself out of his free existential choices rather than defining himself by the stability of an essence.

But psychoanalysis is no more an existentialism than it is a structuralism. The essence of man, if we want to keep this vocabulary, according to the ethics that the existence of psychoanalysis imposes, is to have to answer to structure. It is neither existentialist freedom, nor structural determinism. And the structure about which we are speaking is not that of elementary structures of kinship but that of the effects of language, which is much more basic – real effects, and which are inscribed in the real. As for ethics, it is different from all morals, thus from every normativising position. It is, on the contrary, a position in relation to the real, Lacan said, starting with the 1959–1960 seminar *The Ethics of Psychoanalysis*. Obviously, it is, as always, a question of clarifying what this term "real" encompasses for the psychoanalyst; this term "real" is no more equivocal than any other term. The themes of the seminar indicated clearly which real was at stake: an entire first part consecrated to what Freud introduced with the term drive, then Antigone between two deaths, Sade, the death drive, and even the libertines and their hedonism. This series necessitated the reference to jouissance, introduced using the vocable of the Thing, *das Ding*, and the entire problematic of this extraordinary seminar gets played out between two terms: desire and jouissance.

This is what is latent in the text that I have just quoted and which continues as follows: "Every human formation has as its essence, and not by accident, *the curbing of jouissance* (my italics). The Thing appears naked to us – and no longer through these prisms and lenses called religion, philosophy ... even hedonism, because the pleasure principle is the brake of jouissance" (Lacan, 1967).

We hardly speak any more about the pleasure principle today. We no longer make a big deal about what Lacan brought to light, namely the gap between what the term "pleasure" designates in the Freudian pleasure principle and the notion of pleasure in ancient hedonism, because from one to the other "pleasure changed meaning [*a changé de sens*]", he said. Perhaps I will come back to this, but this phrase – I highlighted this last year – clearly states that what puts the brakes on jouissance is not values. It is not these master signifiers that are the ideals of the Other. The brake is much more structural. It has to do with language itself. Indeed, the Freudian pleasure principle, what is it, under the pen of Freud himself, if not the drift [*dérive*] of drive satisfaction in what he calls "secondary processes", which are nothing other than those of the chain of language? Suffice it to say that the brake that this pleasure principle applies to jouissance does not come from a will for repression of any social or familial Other. It is the destiny of the one who speaks. Said otherwise: Oedipus is at best a myth, but what is not a myth is castration, which is not the effect of the father, which is primary – "primary castration" says the seminar *Anxiety*, because language has a negativising effect on the living individual.

You see how the text on formation is laid out: every formation whatever it may be, no matter which one, is a brake on jouissance, without exception. We understand this because there is not one that does not pass through language. But our worry as psychoanalysts concerns a formation that we can "qualify as human", so not just any formation. How will we be able to define it? Putting the brakes on jouissance, but in a human way? Many questions emerge here that I will have to come back to. Putting on the brakes and repressing, are they one and the same thing? What is the jouissance that must be limited, since there are a lot of them, and is there not some jouissance that, held back, cannot be slowed down – and how can we know how to deal with it?

Without the Other

Freud habituated us to a solution concerning humanising formation: the solution through Oedipus. Lacan continued in the same vein, reformulating it, at least until the end of the *Écrits*. A human formation in this perspective combined the effect of language with the effect of the paternal metaphor, which, if I may say so, is a superimposed effect of discourse, so superimposed that it can fail. Besides, before that, Lacan had essentially posed that a principle of humanisation was to be found in the symbolic, specifically in the symbolic effects of full speech. In both cases, full speech or metaphor, the principle came from the Other with a capital O. We will be able to re-explore this, but Lacan went well beyond. You know the outcome. He concludes by saying, categorically: there is no Other. *Troumatisme*.

Last year, I spoke a little about the thesis of the "generalised child", but only covered it partially. There's much more to it than what I developed then. Whatever one may say, and rightly so, about the child as a subject with rights, the child comes into the world in the position of object *a*. Object of desire or effect of desire, then object of care, with the risk of being the transitional object of the Other unless he is the object of all of its narcissistic projections. But Lacan goes further: all of them, "miscarriages of the desire of the Other". This is not a simple witticism. This signifies clearly that the desire of the Other is responsible for our coming into the world and for our survival – but it is incapable of "bringing us to term" – and thus that our completion as responsible subject – what we call an adult – is not incumbent upon it.

This limit of the Other, which is apparent in the infantile traumatism that Freud described in *Beyond the Pleasure Principle*, arises from this fact. This traumatism is the encounter with an Other who does not respond. "Father don't you see?" This infantile trauma returns in life in the form of repetition, a Freudian thesis, and in analysis where repetition is put back into play, *re-petitio*, it is revealed as being "that which does not cease to be written", the necessary. This is Lacan's big breakthrough: repetition is not the effect of a being's drive but of the structure of the Other of language that constitutes all discourse. In the end, he formulates: "There is no Other." Thus, there remain some others whose discourse presentifies this holed Other, and whose powerlessness to respond, in fact, arises from the impossible. The question is a current one.

Today, the invocation regarding biopower in some way reduplicates infantile trauma. Foucault truly perceived something essential here: today's political power acts in the sense of "making live [*faire vivre*]". Consequently, it reactivates the fantasy of the Other, confronts its powerlessness to satisfy expectations. Henceforth, political power has, in my opinion, the function of "traumatic parent". Lacan uses the expression in the seminar, "Le savoir du psychanalyste" held at Sainte-Anne in 1970. Why the singular, which elides the question of knowing if it's the father or the mother or both, and which elides just as much the question of the sex of this so-called parent? It is, I think, because parent here designates not just any old parent, but the parental function, which consists for adults in being supports, particular incarnations, I could say representatives of the Other, the locus of language and the bearer of discourse. It is the parent as necessarily "*troumatique*", whatever his good intentions may be, or his sex for that matter, because the Other is holed [*troué*]. Which is written S(A̸). So, the invocation, "Father don't you see I'm burning?", which gives the formula of repetition as "missed encounter" that Lacan puts forth in *The Four Fundamental Concepts of Psychoanalysis*, is at present becoming a daily reality, at the conjunction of a destructive and acephalous capitalism on the one side and of a power at the head of the state who is powerless to curb the consequences of it, on the other. Read the press, listen to the radio with this key and you will perceive to what extent this thesis of the generalised child had, for Lacan, a significance that went well beyond every idea of infantilisation. It designated the subjective context of a time, ours, where the symbolic had changed, where the unifying semblants of discourse that once allowed for the compensation of the shortcomings of the Other are no more, where the semblant of the father no long holds the function of Other of the Other. The absence of the Other, the traumatic state, if I could say it like Lacan said, "traumatic parent", "*troumatique*", sets ablaze the call to the Other of *suppléance* [*faire flamber l'appel à l'Autre de suppléance*]. And it is the discourse of contemporary victimisation that at the level of public and political life reanimates the groanings of the traumatic moment of childhood and redoubles them. *Unhappy Identity*, according to Finkielkraut's title. And it is additionally an unprecedented attachment that each of us has to his childhood that, in fact, appears henceforth as the key to everything, as Maurice Gaucher mentions. And also, the developments of so many new and diverse credulities that always aim to reanimate the Other. Anyways, let's move on.

The difference is that infantile trauma is a beneficial trauma. You recognise here a headline that you know, because as painful as it may be, it has effects of separation from the parental Other. I'll not develop them, but they are indeed necessary, although they don't go as far as warding off repetition, the *re-petitio* of the calls to the Other. They are necessary because they open onto the contingency of encounters to come and to the possibility of concluding. Without them, without these effects of separation, we are – just short of the generalised child – in infantilism, which is different. So, can we hope that the *troumatismes* of today have an effect of separation within a civilisation in flux that is homologous to that of the infantile *troumatisme*? This is what we do not yet know. The worries about what we are to encounter are not a good sign. It is a fact however that there is in the current discourse a concern about what we are to encounter. A suspicion about what the policies of the state promise to future generations is well-known, and at the more individual level, a concern about the subjectivity of the children of capitalism. It winds its way into disorder, noise, violence, nostalgia, denunciation – all of this unrest around the new forms of electronic entertainment, of the family, of reproduction, and of couples.

Whatever the issue of the era, it is not the "*troumatique*" Other on whom we can count to bring to term the human formation that Lacan seemed to hope for. Nor is it the full speech of the "you are my woman [*tu es ma femme*]" that leads to the "killed my wife [*tué ma femme*]", nor the father, who is not the Other of the Other as one might have believed with the paternal metaphor. Well?

It occurred to me to say and to write in *Lacan: The Unconscious Reinvented* that Lacan had repudiated his paternal metaphor as well as the metaphor of the symptom as defined in "The instance of the letter in the unconscious". I had – to my own surprise I must say – the occasion to see a colleague jump up when hearing this affirmation about the paternal metaphor, as if it were big news and unacceptable. Maybe she thought, this colleague, that the paternal metaphor was the beyond of Oedipus that Lacan claimed to adhere to. But the paternal metaphor is not Oedipus reinvented, it is only Oedipus reformulated in linguistic terms – thus, it is the same – somewhat rationalised in terms of language. The consequences of Lacan's teaching demand that the question be asked as to what there is in what we call a beyond of Oedipus. What is going to be the principle of humanisation?

It is all of these questions that I plan to take up in detail this year and that I am only introducing today. It is not that they do not still remain somewhat obscure to me. Sometimes I ask myself if there are not some flaws in the coherence of the construction, but, all the same, a certain number of points appear to me to be quite certain and congruent with clinical facts. They are crucial because it is evident that the couple that the metaphor used to organise is in jeopardy today and has ceased to be the dominant model.

The inhuman unconscious

It is indeed logical that the real unconscious [*inconscient réel*], that I write as you know in four initials, RUCS, put into question the paternal metaphor. This unconscious is not in fact a signifying chain but a knowledge [*savoir*] made of *lalangue*, a knowledge to be deciphered, but which remains impregnable, one that we can never entirely catch up to. With it, Lacan could not leave as-is the metaphor of the father, which is a chain, which had as its function the button tie [*point de capiton*] for the entirety of the symbolic order that structures a subject, and which, from its chain, would establish an order between the sexes and the generations. Incidentally, this real unconscious came as a surprise when I published the book that I had consecrated to it. As a result, I have asked myself if for me this book did not fall into the category of what Lacan calls in his logical time "the assertion of anticipated certainty". In any case, since then, I have been in a period of explaining the conclusions that I posed in it.

For the moment, I'll remark only that the notion of this RUCS – which the symptom makes ex-sist in the real, which thus has effects – this notion is in strict solidarity with what Lacan designated as his hypothesis. Thus, it is not surprising that it is evoked in *Encore*, the very seminar in which Lacan makes this hypothesis explicit for the first time, namely that language has effects on that which is not language – the body, a *substance jouissante*.[3] Incidentally, three years after, in the "Preface to the English translation of *Seminar XI*", Lacan says, I quote: "The unconscious (which is not what one believes it to be, I say: the unconscious, being real, if you believe what I say about it)" (Lacan, 2001c, p. 571).[4] Belief is evoked twice. Here, Lacan marks the gap between those who believe in his hypothesis, and then everyone else. What do these others believe, at least those who do not deny the unconscious? I only see one response, they believe in the unconscious as conceptualised by Freud, and even in its first Lacanian translation, namely that this unconscious is a symbolic chain with imaginary effects. The hypothesis says something else: the unconscious is real and it has real effects. What are these effects?

The subject, what Lacan names the subject, and even the divided subject, is the effect supposed to the structure of language, a structure that is always binary, formalised from the opposition/connection S_1/S_2, the generator of meaning. But the effect of unconscious knowledge [*savoir inconscient*] on jouissance is something else. In the response to the second question of "Radiophonie", Lacan says that to follow structure is to follow the "effect of language". The object *a* being the first, major effect of language that Lacan began to construct methodically in the seminar *Anxiety*. There are here two meanings of the word structure. The structure of language, which is well-known, is the chain of metaphor and metonymy – displacement and condensation, said Freud – the chain of all of the tropes of language and of style that linguistics takes for its object of study. And then there is structure as effect of language on the living individual, which generates the object *a* as cause. This is the first effect, not the last. There are others, and they are the very object of psychoanalysis. It's more "linguistery" than linguistics, Lacan says, because it occupies itself with this cause – that which, from language, creates an effect of the (real) unconscious. Again, it must not be forgotten that the effect of language passes through speech articulated in language. This unconscious owes nothing to transference. It is for all who speak, whether they know it or not. It has always ex-sisted. I quote *Télévision*: "The unconscious has always spoken." It is not elucubrated, it is encountered, and it has effects, irreducible ones.

Now, this RUCS, constitutive of man, it is indeed difficult, whatever that which is proper to man may be, to qualify it as human if by this qualifier we mean that which renders relations between humans possible and liveable. Indeed, it only presides, to sum it up, over the damage [*dégâts*] proper to man: the paradoxes of desire, the ever unsatisfied and often dissident demands of the drive, partial, parcelled, and castrated jouissances (Lacan says this, echoing the term castration introduced by Freud), the unary fixations of the symptom – in sum, the impossible that announces, "There is no such thing as a sexual relationship", and which is the real "proper" (Lacan, 1975b, p. 17) to the unconscious. Today it is redoubled in the real proper to capitalism which can be said: "There is no such thing as a social link." With that, one understands that the torment of psychoanalysts could be, as Lacan said, that of a formation which we may qualify as human. Hence the question: if we have to give up on the oedipal show continuing to be the main attraction [*s'il faut renoncer à ce que l'Œdipe continue à tenir l'affiche*] – and this is the case – said otherwise, if we have to give up on resorting to the oedipal metaphor, what is it then that will be able to humanise if not the real unconscious, or at least the no less real effects of it on those who speak?

Notes

1 [*l'humanitairerie de commande dont s'habillent nos exactions.*]
2 [In French *humain* means both human and humane. Likewise, *inhumain* means both inhuman and inhumane. In what follows, it should be noted that every instance of *humain* or *inhumain* has been translated according to context.]
3 [The French word jouissance is derived from the verb *jouir*. Here, with *jouissante*, we find the present participle of this verb, indicating that the body is a substance that is actively engaged in jouissance. Throughout this text, we translate *jouir* in its various

forms as "enjoy", whereas jouissance is left untranslated and is not italicised. It must be noted, however, that *jouir* does not imply simple enjoyment, but connotes both sexual orgasm and a dimension of suffering.]

4 [This translation differs from the introduction found in Alan Sheridan's translation of *Seminar XI*. The French text reads: *"l'inconscient (qui n'est ce qu'on croit, je dis: l'inconscient, soit réel, qu'à m'en croire)."*]

Chapter II

27th November 2013

I left you with the question of knowing what can produce a truly human formation. What is to be humanised is man as an animal denatured by the effects of the unconscious on the real, of the unconscious that is also real because it is made of *lalangue*, which is outside meaning. Lacan did not cease to make progress on this question. He started with the paternal metaphor which supposed that the father was necessary, going up to the schema of the Borromean knot that he introduced, and not by accident, at the very moment where he says, "the real unconscious" and where he formulates his hypothesis. These three steps are simultaneous and solidary. Lacan awaited an answer to the question of the humanisation that can go through the father, but doesn't necessarily have to. This answer, crucial for our time must be opened up, but also evaluated. This is what I will attempt to do after following the steps leading up to it.

The denatured

I will start again with the notion of humanisation, a notion whose contours I must trace. Let us begin with the fact that this notion supposes the prerequisite of the brake that is put on jouissance in a structural way, as Lacan mentioned at the conclusion of the 1969 *Journées* on the subject of children and psychosis. What curbs [jouissance] at first, if not semblants, the ideals of culture or of religion, is the passage through the defiles of language, in short, the operation of the signifier, what Freud names the "secondary processes" which condition the pleasure principle. It is certain that the pleasure principle, far from being a jouissance principle, is a principle of less jouissance which enters into opposition with the pressure of the demands of the drive, and which manages to mark bodily excitation just as much as it does the pressure of superego imperatives. This is why Lacan said that the pleasure principle is to do as little as possible. It is a limitation principle and not a jouissance principle. The paragraph from Lacan that I cited is composed of two strata: the entry into language produces jouissance as already curbed, and it is on top of this that a human formation must be placed. It is not a question of a humanisation of a natural being as Jean-Jacques Rousseau seems to have imagined it. I said *seems* because I think that, in fact, he only pretended that the Emile of his treatise on education was the infantile version of the good savage that he placed at the origin of societies. But this was only a heuristic myth, a theoretical fable forged for the purposes of thinking. I am thus going to begin with denaturing. It consists, on the one hand, in being made a subject, and on the other, in receiving a body for jouissance.

As soon as the child enters into language, jouissance is produced at the same time that it is curbed. We often have a tendency to imagine that jouissance is a phenomenon of life. We even authorise ourselves to support this idea with the phrase from Lacan: "In order to enjoy [*jouir*], a body is necessary." Yes, but it is not a sufficient condition. Everything that we imagine concerning the body outside of language – and we only imagine it – everything that we imagine that a body outside of language experiences, or can experience, such as hunger, thirst, pain, etc., all of this cannot be ascribed to jouissance in Lacan's sense of the word. Jouissance is something experienced, certainly, but which is modified by the operation of the signifier. This is why at the beginning of "La troisième", Lacan introduces the question of knowing if the purring of the cat and the purring of language are the same thing, and later on he asks himself if the plant enjoys [*jouit*]. The fact is, jouissance is not simply a phenomenon of life. The jouissance of which we speak in psychoanalysis supposes what is living [*le vivant*], but it is jouissance "civilised" by *lalangue* that gives it its developed form. In any case, it is extremely difficult to speak about jouissance because "jouissance is a limit" as Lacan says in *Encore*, a limit precisely because what is experienced is heterogeneous to language, but it is only approached, even in practice, by way of language.

Structure, Lacan says in "Radiophonie", is the effect of language. There are different strata of this denaturing operation, which Lacan described on many occasions, coming back to the same examples each time he added something – for example, with the *Fort/Da* but also with Freud's Hans case, which has often been commented on. It's hard to give a summary of it here, but we can distinguish the primary effect of symbolisation from the effect of the signifying chain, which is already something else and which I can call "the subject effect", properly speaking. These are real effects of the symbolic. And then there is the effect on the body, producer of jouissance, and here, these are effects of the symbolic on the real of what is living [*du vivant*], which is something else entirely. Lacan started by developing the first of these, but they go together, and this is what the formula of his hypothesis indicates: this formula says that the individual – and the individual is the body – the individual affected by language is the same as the one that he calls the subject.

Real effects of the symbolic

I will begin with the first symbolisation, with the example, so often cited, of Freud's grandson, at the moment where he symbolises the absence of his mother with the alternation of two phonemes, and the fact that they are mispronounced does not prevent them from having the differential structure of the signifier. Here it is not a question of language as a chain but of the minimal binary cell of two signifiers, the one that is missing for certain autistic children who play repetitively with alternating actions: switch on/switch off, open/close, but without any effect of symbolisation. With the *Fort/Da* the mother will never quite be there as she was before. Reciprocally, her presence will be maintained in her absence, and she will never again be all that absent either. Hence the sometimes-fervent efforts of the analysand to get rid of her ... From this moment on, the real relation to the primordial object is holed [*trouée*]. The symbol is the "murder of the Thing", it has a "function of *irréalisation*", Lacan will say again in "On a question prior to any possible treatment of psychosis". At the point where Lacan introduces the Borromean knot, when he says that language makes a hole in the real, we seem to be dealing with the same theme of a negativising effect, but the question is to know if it is the same.

Freud approached the negativising effect of the signifier, albeit in different terms, at the end of his *Interpretation of Dreams* in the passage where he describes how indestructible desire is engendered beginning with a first mythical, hallucinatory experience of satisfaction, which itself would be real, not marked, not holed. The memory trace that it leaves makes of it a definitively lost experience because the only possible reunion that remains is a reunion with the trace, and desire is constituted from the loss that is produced.

Moreover, there is the effect of speech, producer of the want-to-be subject [*sujet manque à être*], who is itself an effect of the signifying chain, which is not the simple minimal binary I was just speaking about. The entire construction of the graph is based on the presupposition that the chain is the generator of the want-to-be, with the idea that desire finds its first foundation in this want-to-be. Let us say about desire that it is the only being of the subject, the only being of a want-to-be subject. When we talk about the being of the subject, we are talking about desire. This thesis is not suspended by the end of Lacan's teaching. Let me remind you that up until *Encore*, when he formulates his hypothesis, he says, "The subject turns out to be – and this is only true for speaking beings – a being [*un étant*] whose being is always elsewhere, as the predicate shows" (Lacan, 1999, p. 142). The reference to the predicate is a reference to the chain in which the predicate is the second signifier, with which we are attempting, but in a recurring and endless way, to respond to the question about what the subject is. A little before he had stated: "a subject doesn't have much to do with jouissance", "he is presumed in an articulated sentence, in something that is organised or can be organised on the basis of a whole life" (Lacan, 1999, p. 50). Notice that it is the sentence that is organised by life and not life that is organised by the sentence. Would this be an existentialist thesis? I don't think so; it's rather that a sentence is only constituted by its button tie [*point de capiton*], and that for life, it is death that eventually makes it possible to read the sentence.

Nevertheless, it is necessary to adjust the vocabulary of lack [*manque*] and of loss. I am not going to do a systematic study of this theme – that could be a thesis because there is a certain confusion about it. In the formulations, Lacan first of all talked about lack, but in the end, this notion of lack is ambiguous, oscillating between want-to-be – this is the first formula – and want-to-enjoy [*manque à jouir*], which is connoted by the term castration, and Lacan symbolises both the want-to-be and the loss that constitutes castration with the same signifier, the phallus.

The want-to-be is a phenomenon of the subject, of that which is supposed to the signifier [*du supposé au signifiant*]. It is inherent to the one who speaks, who, from the fact that he speaks, does not know where his being is, always lost as he is between signifiers. The question of being is at the origin of analysis because the want-to-be implies the want-to-know [*manque à savoir*], and it is this lack, moreover, that is the generator of love, I mean of the demand for love, which is always a demand for being, the passion for being. We are here in the phenomena of the subject.

The loss, on the other hand, certainly concerns the subject but it has more to do with the real, and specifically the real of the body. Think about the myth of Adam's rib, a rib that is lost and then found again in an unexpected form. Think about the pound of flesh that one has to pay. See also how Lacan in the *Four Fundamental Concepts of Psychoanalysis* and in "Position of the unconscious" connects it to the fact of sexed reproduction and evokes it as a part of life that is subtracted owing to the fact of this reproduction linked to individual death. This has nothing to do with any subject whatsoever – and he illustrates it with the placenta, with envelopes, with decidua [*caduques*], from which the child is separated at birth, and even with the lizard who, in distress, loses the end of its tail. In fact, the loss designates what produces the object *a*. The right word is subtraction of the object *a*, the one that he develops and constructs throughout the seminar *Anxiety*, as an effect of the Other, as locus of the signifier, on the "natural" subject. The subject is not only a want-to-be. He is divided by this object that causes him, and Lacan produces three consecutive schemas of this division, which in some ways overdetermines his definition of both the subject and desire. In the *Fort/Da* we spoke about the symbolisation of the mother, but it concerned just as much the child as individual, who is no less constituted as an effect of language than is his primordial object. But once he produces the object *a*, Lacan is able to reread the case and highlight that, in tossing the spool over the railing of his crib, it is himself that he makes disappear. In some respect, he plays with the subtraction that constitutes him as a subject.

The being of the subject, desire, is doubly determined, both by the production of the want-to-be and by the loss. Lacan indicates this in the "The direction of the treatment" with a paradoxical expression – desire is "an aporia incarnate". I quote: in this "aporia incarnate – of which one might metaphorically say that demand borrows its heavy soul from the hardy offshoots of the wounded tendency, and its subtle body from death as it is actualised in the signifying sequence" (Lacan, [1958a] 2006, p. 525). The heavy soul of desire comes from the object of the drives – prettily named here "offshoots of the wounded tendency", that is to say, need – and its subtle body from the negativisation mobilised by the body of the symbolic. Here is what condenses the subject effect to the effect on the body. Desire comes from the Other, it is desire of the Other, but its cause comes from the carnal subtraction. And here we enter into another chapter, not the one about the production of the subject by the symbolic, but the one about the effects of the symbolic on what is living [*le vivant*].

These effects result from the fact that the symbolic takes on a body. In the past, in my commentary on Question II of "Radiophonie", I insisted on the fact that we generally comment on the thesis of the body that incorporates the symbolic, or of the symbolic that is incorporated, whichever you prefer. Hence the expression the body, locus of the Other, or "the body paves the way for the Other [*le corps fait le lit de l'Autre*]". I'll come back to this. But we make less noise about the affirmation that comes just before this, where Lacan says that structure is caught, and I quote, "beginning with the point where the symbolic takes on a body", or alternatively constitutes itself as a body. Suffice it to say that the symbolic could not take on a body or that in itself, it does not have a body. "What has a body and yet does not exist?" Lacan asked. Answer: the big Other. If I ask: what exists and yet has no body? I can answer *lalangue*. In 1970, Lacan was not yet emphasising *lalangue,* but we grasp retrospectively that a language [*langue*] in the idiomatic sense, is a symbolic that has no body – symbolic because it is made of linguistic elements, but which are not incorporated. The only place where a language seems to be assembled, made like a body, is the dictionary where it is gathered, but the dictionary, I said, is a graveyard. You understand then why Lacan says that every language, even when it is in use, is a dead language – deadwood, he says: it is because it is made of the past, of verbal traces of the living experiences of a community. On the other hand, the unconscious-*lalangue* of the one who speaks is always in the present, because it is of incorporated *lalangue* that has passed into language [*langage*], if by language we actually mean some enjoyed signifier [*signifiant joui*]. So then, it would be more accurate to say about a language [*langue*], not that it does not have a body, but that it lost that which gave a body of jouissance to its signifying elements – namely living bodies – where, from being incorporated, incarnated, it itself became a body. And this provides the justification for saying that each of us has his own *lalangue*. All of this is to remind you that to the real effects of the symbolic, and to the effect of the symbolic on the real, Lacan yet added the symbolic elevated to the real of jouissance, which is the major thesis of the seminar *Encore* and which really shakes things up.

Effects on the real

Lacan gave two essential models of this effect of language [*langage*]: the genesis of the drives and the genesis of the symptom.

What is striking is that the genesis of the drives is established quite early and definitively. We notice it in "Remarks on Daniel Lagache's presentation" and "The subversion of the subject and the dialectic of desire", then in *Seminar XI* and "Position of the unconscious". After this, there's no going back on this model.

As far as the symptom is concerned, things are different. Let us say it begins with "The instance of the letter in the unconscious". Lacan had spoken before about the symptom in "The function and field of speech and language", and even in what he calls "On my antecedents", especially concerning the mirror stage, but it is here that he gives the first formula of the symptom as a language formation, specifically as a metaphor constructed on the signifier of trauma. Following this, he never stopped reworking his conception of the symptom and rethinking its function, right up until the end. *R.S.I.* situates it not as a metaphor but as a letter, in which jouissance has happened upon a signifier which makes a letter of it – an event of the RUCS – and Lacan continues elaborating its function throughout the final seminars.

The first model then, the passage from need to the drives (Lacan, [1960a] 2006, p. 548), dates from the 1960s. Before the saying of the demand finds its echo in the body in the form of the drive, we cannot talk about jouissance but only about need and satisfaction, hunger and repletion, for example. But when by excitation of the oral zone, the body responds to, echoes, the injunction to absorb, which comes from the Other, then we can talk about jouissance. And it is clear that it is at once limited and localised, which is why we say partial drive, but its exigency is from then on impossible to stop. The drives, however, can be diverted [*dérivées*]. This is why they have two modes of being realised: either they take action [*passent à l'acte*], or they drift [*dérivent*] and are metonymised in the business of sublimation, and Lacan gets it right when he says about this in *The Ethics of Psychoanalysis* that it is nothing other than displacement. When Lacan says, "I speak with my body" and without knowing it, the best illustration that we can give of it is the drives that effectively say what "I" want – I have already developed this. With the drives, the subject makes his entrance into the real. Leading up to this echo in the body, the subject was in the symbolic, the subject about which we spoke but which itself did not speak, not even with its body. Here, the subject begins to speak with his body. I won't insist on this further.

As for the symptom, I have chosen to spend some time on what Lacan says about it in 1975, in the Geneva conference, "Le symptôme". The text concerns the genesis, not of the drives, but of symptoms, of "enjoying" the symptom [*"se jouit" du symptôme*], and it is contemporaneous with the concept of RUCS. I have realised that, where phobia is concerned, it allows for a dovetailing of his first theses and his later ones. The symptom "enjoys [*se jouit*]" is originally a Freudian thesis, although the definition of the symptom isn't exactly the same. The first manifest difference with the drives is that the symptom does not drift [*dérive*], is not metonymised. On the contrary, it is characterised by its inertia. It creates a *fixion* of jouissance, fiction with an *x*. However, one common trait, from the drive to the symptom, is the function of a first saying in their constitution. In order to give an account of the symptom, Lacan reaffirms the linguistic determination of jouissance which leads him to a formula of the symptom as "coalescence of sexual reality and original language". Lacan says: "It is at an early period that there is crystallised for the child what has to be called by its name, namely symptoms.

The period of childhood is decisive in this respect" (Lacan, 1985, p. 10). For those who have read *Encore*, how would this coalescence not evoke what he has said there: the signifier, knowledge [*le savoir*], enjoys [*se jouit*]. It is a formula of coalescence. For the symptom, it is not the saying of the demand or of the supply that operates as it does with the drives. These are the words of *lalangue* carried by the discourse of the parents, some words or elements; he says "detritus", "debris" deposited by the bath of language where the child has been received, in order to make the point that these are ones [*des uns*], elements outside of the chain, and which constitute the *motérialité* of his unconscious. This is a first point, a well-established one. The unconscious is effectively approached word for word in the Freudian technique by means of dreams, slips, bungled actions, and what the analysand says [*dits de l'analysant*]. But the words of the symptom have a meaning – Lacan refers here to Freud's *Introductory Lectures on Psychoanalysis* – and this meaning comes from the first experiences, that is to say the first encounters with "sexual reality", namely jouissance. What he calls sexual reality here is not the drives about which he had said in *The Four Fundamental Concepts of Psychoanalysis* that they were the sexual reality of the unconscious. Here we are concerned with another reality. I quote, that of "the encounter certain beings have with their own erection". Note that this is only concerning the masculine side of the matter. This erection, Lacan contests that it is autoerotic as Freud said, from the fact that the child discovers it on his own body. It is "hetero", not in the sense of hetero-sexuality but in the sense of strangeness. It is the strangeness of a real.

His model here is Little Hans, who is so afraid of it that he forges the symptom of his phobia in response to this excess of real. "Phobia means that he is terrified of it [*il en a la trouille*]". At this moment, we could talk about the penis as traumatic for him.

This example of Hans is rather propitious for perceiving the gap between what we call phallic jouissance and penile jouissance. The latter, penile jouissance, is only elevated to phallic jouissance by the operation of language, when it acquires a function in the symbolic. Phallic jouissance is not outside of the symbolic, it is outside of the body, Lacan says. Outside of the body in the sense that the body is the imaginary, the form of the body, the sack. The drives are at the surface; phallic jouissance is outside of the body. Look where Lacan writes it in the layout of the Borromean knot, between S and R, outside of the imaginary. It is "hetero" with respect to the body, but not foreign to the subject of the signifier and even so not foreign that it supports it in its entire relationship to reality. This is why Lacan gave a new formula for the superego, the superego that Freud thought to be the interdictor, and Lacan says that its imperative is: *enjoy* [*joui*]. This is quite logical: the interdictor of pleasures that pushes for civilising efforts, according to Freud. And so, Lacan says in *Encore* that its ironic commandment in fact prescribes phallic jouissance, the one at stake in every undertaking of civilisation, the one that shouldn't be in order to be fulfilled.

I'll return to the example: so, we have Hans's phobia, a symptom and an interpretation, which says the meaning of this symptom. The meaning of this symptom is the rejection of this erectile jouissance. Note that the meaning is not given by jouissance alone, but by the position of Hans with regard to this real erection – a position with respect to a real. I call it real not because it comes from the organism, although it does. It is real because it is outside the symbolic, more precisely outside the symbolic to which Hans has access, and this from the fact that nothing in the discourse of the family permits him to situate it, to give it a function. And Lacan says, I quote: "He understands exactly nothing, thanks to the fact, of course, that he has a certain kind of mother and a certain kind of father" (Lacan, 1985, p. 15). Said otherwise, this symptom is linked to the parental truth.

Here, I could add: surprise. Why does Lacan, in order to explain the genesis of the symptom, come back to one of the first symptoms that he commented on, child phobia, and furthermore, why does he do so in evoking his first developments from the seminar *La relation d'objet*? I say, "come back to" because we are in 1975, after he introduced, in *Encore,* the new and crucial thesis of the signifier that enjoys [*se jouit*], and after *R.S.I.* – that is to say, after he reformulated his definition of the symptom, no longer as a metaphor but as a real, enjoyed letter [*lettre jouie réelle*], with no connection to the truth of the subject. In doing so, he makes the unconscious ex-sist in the real. This definition of the symptom separated it from subjective truth. And so, I think that it is quite instructive for us and that it is not only didactic because he is speaking to analysts of the IPA. And I am going to show you how the example of phobia enters into his later theses, just as much as the obsession of the Rat Man, which I talked about last year.

With this phobia, Lacan chooses a symptom, let's say a classic one, and he comments on it in terms that are well-known to his readers. The symptom of Hans, who is a child, echoes the parental truth. This is what the phrase that I have just quoted says. He does not talk about the letter of the symptom but about what he said in "Science and truth", that the symptom has truth as its cause, and since it is a child who is concerned here, his truth still remains knotted to that of his parents. Apparently, this is not the symptom as real and in the real, of the years surrounding 1975. Let us take a closer look.

Phobia is a very particular symptom. He always situated it in this way. It demonstrates a basic mechanism, namely how, confronted with an unbearable real, the subject invokes what I can designate as a defence by means of the symbolic in subsuming the real – here, the unthinkable erection – under a random signifier, the horse. Thus, the real in question, it is quite clear, is not the one that shows itself to be the impossible of the relationship, the one that Lacan named a real proper to the unconscious. It is, on the contrary, a real that is encountered, the same that Lacan writes as one of the rings of the Borromean knot. It is a real outside of the symbolic. So, this means that phobia is an intersection of the real and the symbolic. This was the first thesis of Lacan concerning phobia, and it was original: there where one generally has the idea that in phobia, the imaginary flares up with its bestiary and all of its representations of dangerous figures, Lacan made a correction in saying that, in essence, whatever the figure may be, it is an "all-purpose signifier [*signifiant à tout faire*]" inasmuch as it connotes danger. Phobia is a signifier convoked for the purposes of representing a traumatic real, that is to say, without a signifier. This structure is the minimum basis of the symptom such as it is defined in "The instance of the letter in the unconscious". The symptom is a metaphor that substitutes "the enigmatic signifier of sexual trauma" for another signifier. The signifier of phobia, such as it is illustrated in the case of Hans, is the homologue of this first signifier, before any substitution whatsoever, except that it is not a simple memory index or a unary trait, but rather a product of the unconscious that realises a displacement from the real to the symbolic.

    I have not reached the end of my development. I will pick it back up the next time.

Chapter III

11th December 2013

I am in the process of showing the conception Lacan had of the typical forms of jouissance "fitted out [*appareillée*]" by language, which are the drives and symptoms. I stopped last time at this basic symptom of phobia, to which Lacan returns in the conference "Le symptôme", from October 1975, just after *R.S.I.* and before the famous seminar *Le Sinthome*.

I have already highlighted that phobia operates a "displacement of the real into the symbolic" (Lacan, 1970, p. 72).

Jouissance, fitted out

Lacan often came back to this: on the last page of the *Écrits* he refers to it as the "abyss against which he" – the subject – "protects himself with a phobia" (Lacan, [1966] 2006, p. 745). The abyss is the mother's absence of a penis. Hans's traumatic penis is not without making a reference to it. This is quite obvious in the entire observation of the case. But he comes back to it, above all, in the "Compte rendu de l'acte analytique". I will read the passage: "The unconscious means that there is some knowledge without a subject. The idea of instinct crushes this discovery: but the discovery survives from the fact that knowledge never turns out to be anything but readable. The front line of resistance depends upon this work that is as excessively elaborate as a phobia can be" (Lacan, 1984b, p. 19).

Now, let me comment on this. "Knowledge without a subject" is the paradoxical formula that I situate as the embryo of the RUCS, not of the real proper to the unconscious as Lacan says, which is the non-relationship, but of the unconscious that one can call real, and well before the "Preface to the English language edition of *Seminar XI*", because it is not a signifying chain but is made of elements of *lalangue* which ultimately presentify this knowledge without a subject, and it is a knowledge that determines, not the subject, but his jouissance. Lacan says it just after.

The instinct of animals functions, at least in our eyes, as some knowledge in the real, because everything happens as though they already knew what they have to do in order to survive and reproduce. We could then confuse the unconscious, this Other, extimate to those who speak, with instinct, but the difference is that, by definition, knowledge is read [*ça se lit*], from the verb *lire* (to read).

Phobia resists the possible reduction of the unconscious to instinct because phobia makes use of the signifier, which is read and which therefore takes on a meaning from the context in which it has fixed itself. For Hans, the meaning is given by refusal of the jouissance of the organ. So why "an excessively elaborate work?" Work [*ouvrage*] evokes forging just as much as the term "formations of the unconscious" does, and phobia moves forward there where there is some real, that is to say, there where there is no signifier, but only a frightening real. It moves forward in order to put into place some signifier, any signifier, equalling the signifier of the traumatic real. In other words, it is quite clear, phobia makes the passage from the real to the signifier. This can be written: S_1/R, a sort of primary metaphor. This is the way that Lacan first thought of it. With phobia, we could already have talked about the *motérialité* of the unconscious, before Lacan creates this term, because it is a basic unit of the *motérialité* of the unconscious. This is most likely why, as time went on, Lacan stopped making a clinical structure of it.

Motérialité

Lacan came to modify his concept of the unconscious as a *motérialité* without a signifying chain – words, but without metaphor – and explicitly so, if we wish to be good readers, when he says: "Contrary to what I said in 'The function and field of speech and language', in the unconscious, words do not make a chain." Consequently, if they do not make a chain, the unconscious is necessarily real: made of words, let us say more generally, made of elements that are outside of a chain, outside of meaning because meaning convokes the imaginary, and, moreover ... that are enjoyed – because this is the new definition of knowledge, introduced in *Encore*: knowledge is made up of the signifier that enjoys [*se jouit*]. So, when in this conference Lacan presents the example of phobia as the illustration of what he calls "the coalescence of the *motérialité* of the unconscious with sexual reality" – that is to say, with phallic jouissance – couldn't this mean that phobia is the primary clinical example, the major example, of a symptom that makes exsist some RUCS, as *motérialité* outside of a chain? Phobia operates a transfer of the anxiety [*angoisse*] produced by the burgeoning activity of the organ – let us say, by penile jouissance – to the signifier of the horse, and let me point out that this signifier is not a signifier that is borrowed from the discourse of the parents. But in doing so, Hans's horse, champing at the bit, just like the Rat Man's rat, becomes the object of fascination, and condenses all sorts of representations; it is not only a symbol of danger, it is quite noticeable that it is itself an object of excitation, of jouissance, then, which could be written without forcing the matter, like Lacan writes the letter of the symptom in *R.S.I.*, $f(x)$, jouissance of an element of the unconscious.

Lacan used to say that phobia is a "hub [*plaque tournante*]". This signifies that it can lead in different directions: either towards a series of associated signifiers, or not, and if not, we remain at the coalescence of a signifier and jouissance, like Lacan writes the symptom in *R.S.I.* Phobia leads as much to a possible signifying substitution as to the letter, the letter that psychosis does not exclude. Indeed, there are phobias not only in neurosis, but also in psychosis – real ones, with a phobic signifier. "An all-purpose signifier", Lacan says, for creating metaphor as much as the letter – which does not prevent us from giving it some meaning based on the position of the subject with respect to a real, in the context where it is produced, as Lacan does for Hans.

Another notable fact concerning phobia: it is a transitory symptom for most children, and there must be a reason for this. The reason is that jouissance "fitted out" by phobia is not just any old jouissance. It is not the jouissance of the partial drives, phallic jouissance, the one that can find its place in the sexed relation of bodies. Phobia is a sort of typical symptom of the moment of the crossing of what Freud called the "castration complex" – which, as Lacan says, is not so complex – but which is the moment where this "hetero" jouissance is encountered and where it is a question of finding a function for it. At this moment in childhood, the sexual theories of children no longer suffice, those which used to convoke precisely the jouissance of the partial drives in order to imagine what goes on between adults when they are in the bedroom. Hence, the idea of the scene called primal, oral, anal, sadistic, etc., for making babies. With this new organ of jouissance – let's put it that way – the penis, new with respect to the erogenous zones of the partial drives, the question is renewed. What purpose does this serve when we are two sexed bodies in the bedroom and no longer only one body with its options … for masturbation. When I speak of the function of the organ, this refers to its role in jouissance but also in procreation, the great enigma for children if we believe what Freud says about it. Obviously, the couple that the child has before his eyes and whose speech he hears and interprets is going to grant him the more or less easy reduction of anxiety [*angoisse*]. This reduction of anxiety comes from the response to the question of knowing what he can do with this organ, or just as well, to the question of how one can do without it when one doesn't have it – thus, it comes from the function that the organ receives from the couple in the biographical context of the moment. The adult couple functions here as an example of a response that is more or less favourable according to whether or not it enables the child to anticipate the future function of this organ when he grows up. And I'll have you notice that the function of this couple will not be less if it is a question of a homosexual couple because the phallus, signifier of jouissance, is not any less in its place than in the heterosexual couple. It is obvious when it's a male couple, and when it's a female couple, it shows, on the contrary, that it can be the phallus without the organ – all things that Freud obviously never considered. Neither is it necessary that this be the couple of the progenitors of the traditional family, given that this couple in the relation with the child assures the parental function, which consists, I said, in presentifying the Other in the here and now.

What fostered the insistent anxiety of Hans? Lacan says: he was missing the example of a father who "fucks the mother". In my opinion, this remark has generated a lot of misunderstanding. Indeed, we know that in the couple there was a mother who did not let herself be fucked, and Lacan knew this from Freud. So, can we imagine that Lacan thought that it was necessary that he force her? No, he (Hans) lacked the example of a couple where the organ took on its phallic meaning, its meaning as an organ of jouissance and of procreation. When Lacan takes up the example of Hans in "The instance of the letter in the unconscious", he formulates things differently. He says that Hans was "left in the lurch", an expression from Schreber, left in the lurch by "the shortcomings [*carences*] of his symbolic entourage". But the question to ask is: what is the relation between the carnal union of the couple and the symbolic? For the Lacan of that time, it was obvious and logical given his thesis concerning the oedipal metaphor because according to him, it conditioned the hetero-sexual couple, the father being what I called the mediator of the phallus as the sexual lack of the mother in the place of Other. It is very explicit in *La relation d'objet*, in the writing of the paternal metaphor and in all the texts that follow. He went back on this thesis. I have explained this.

Let me conclude on the constitution of the symptom as it is thus presented in this conference from 1975. In the coalescence, this time of *motérialité* and of sexual reality, the latter is obviously the one of sexual difference, I would even say, of phallic jouissance. Lacan even adds that the invention of the unconscious by Freud is linked to this phallic jouissance. A question can be raised concerning the two jouissances that are fitted out by language, drive jouissance and symptom jouissance: how do they hook into one another, and what is their role in sexuality? The first is connected to desire. Lacan said in 1964 in *The Four Fundamental Concepts of Psychoanalysis* that the object cause of desire is the object of the drive. Drive jouissance is in play in the fantasy, which props up desire and where the object is placed; on the other hand, in the symptom, it is phallic jouissance that is fixed. Have a look at the knot that Lacan draws in the supplement to the lesson of December 17th 1974, in *R.S.I.* In the layout of the tripartite Borromean knot, he writes phallic jouissance at the intersection between the Symbolic and the Real, and the symptom as an overflow of this intersection onto the real. This creates a difference with the jouissance of fantasy, which is in fact *joui-sens*, implying the imaginary, and the jouissance of the symptom, which is phallic jouissance extracted from the symbolic.

It must indeed appear to you that all of these effects of the language apparatus – whether it be a matter of desire or of these two forms of "civilised" jouissance that are the drives and the symptom – are not as civil as all that. The speaking-being [*parlêtre*] would be a wandering being whose being is always elsewhere if he did not have a body that moored him – that's for sure. Only, more is necessary than this body of drive and symptomatic jouissance in order for the one who speaks to make community [*fasse société*], so that, without even evoking the *affectio societatis*, he puts up with his semblables enough to at least live next to them peacefully. In saying "live next to", I am not even talking about the social link [*lien social*] because capitalism has taught us that we can ensure the neighbourhood and the connections between bodies and even masses of bodies, which would not be a social link, in the sense of a social order, and which would only be the aggregate, generator of segregation. I have developed this point at length in previous years.

What destiny – and maybe it is necessary to use the plural – what possible destinies does the double operation of the *corporisation* of the symbolic and its incorporation in the flesh – with these three effects that are desire, drive, and symptom – lay out for the one who speaks?

Object a, the orphan

I will begin with what I might call the incivility of desire. It seems necessary to me to make a clarification regarding this notion of desire, one of the terms that psychoanalysis, following Freud, borrowed from common language. Lacan did not place it among the fundamental concepts of psychoanalysis. He did, however, make a big deal about it. In Lacanian psychoanalysis, we have idealised desire a great deal. Lacan induced this effect, certainly, but he also challenged it, asking in 1975 at the *Journée des cartels* whether or not psychoanalysis was going to become the religion of desire. Where did this idealisation come from that has subsequently culminated in an idealisation of the desire of the analyst?

We can link it to the first conception of desire that Lacan constructed, starting with his first seminars. It's worth having a close look at the dates because Lacan's elaborations advanced very quickly. The "Direction of the treatment" had been delivered in July of 1958 in Royaumont, (not published until 1961) just before "Desire and its interpretation". This text made desire the target of the analytic operation and made the phallus, signifier of desire, the sole compass of interpretation. Moreover, the neurotic was characterised by a desire that was questionable and unstable in its problematic, a desire that one would hope to firm up by means of analysis. Desire was thus situated as an analytic value [*valeur analytique*]. In the texts that follow, we have to think about the developments on Hamlet and his desire that recoils before the act, and this with the question of knowing what was able to correct this procrastination. Think about Antigone two years later in *The Ethics of Psychoanalysis:* the heroine of desire, opposed to the ethics of goods. And, at the end of this same seminar, think about the famous theme of "giving ground relative to one's desire", etc. I'm not giving an exhaustive account here. We will most likely do this at the next international meeting dedicated to the "Paradoxes of desire". But it is obvious that desire in Lacanian discourse has become something like an analytic value. We were not then at the point of what he said much later about psychoanalysis, that it is a practice without value, which does not mean that it is worthless but rather that it does not have recourse to any value whatsoever. And when we speak now about the real, the real itself should not be invoked as a value.

"La proposition sur le psychanalyste de l'École" is built upon this thesis of the value of desire. The final operation [*opération de la fin*] being to make it possible to transform a singular desire, one that is fixed on a specified fantasmatic object, into the desire of the analyst, and this is not simply the desire of an analyst, but a desire that must be an operator [*opérateur*] of the analytic cure. Lacan talks about the clarification of this new desire. I remind you of these well-known theses, which have been heavily commented on and so often repeated. They lead to defining the analyst by means of a modality of desire, which reinforces the temptation of idealisation, even the heroising of desire. And so, as a result, it is probably not that surprising that the RUCS, which implies an entirely different thing, isn't easy to swallow [*ne passe pas comme une lettre à la poste*] for certain readers of Lacan.

Only, it is quite necessary to measure that the very conception of desire in Lacan evolved and was not achieved in one fell swoop. In the first texts and for a long time after, during the whole of the *Écrits,* desire is situated by the (lowercase) phallic signifier [*signifiant phallus*], the signifier of the Other's lack. Only, this notion of lack is ambiguous. Although Lacan first comments on it as a want-to-be [*manque à être*] inherent to the subject, it also designates, starting with Freud (and so before Lacan), the lack of castration, which is not a want-to-be but a want-to-enjoy [*manque à jouir*], which puts us, not on the side of the subject, but on the side of the living body. The problem is that Lacan first used the same phallic signifier for these two heterogeneous lacks. Additionally, he gave to this signifier a sexuating function, if I may say so, since it permitted the distributing of the two sexes into a "being the phallus" and a "having the phallus". It is with this then that Lacan attempted to organise the entire field of the sexual, of the semblants of sex, and of sexual desire. The cases developed in "The direction of the treatment" all went in this direction – the case of the beautiful butcher's wife as much the fresh brains man, which Lacan borrowed from analytic literature, or the case of the three-card monte man with which Lacan made his own contribution. However, let us note that he did not say "the phallus cause of desire". It would be more like "reason for desire", because it is indeed the phallic lack that is supposed to prop up the vector of sexuated desire.

When Lacan says of the object *a*, "*l'(a)cause première* of desire" (Lacan, 1975a, p. 8),[1] let us ask ourselves if this changes anything, and if so, what? Let me remind you of the thesis such as he formulates it in the short text titled "... ou pire", published at the beginning of *Scilicet 5* in 1975: "As for me, I say that knowledge affects the body of the being, [...] up to the point of producing the scraps [*chutes*] from which I make the (*a*), to be read *objet petit a* [...] or even *l'(a)cause première* of his desire."[2] So this fallen object is "that which is lacking" (Lacan, 1998c, p. ix), as he says in 1976 in the "Preface to the English language edition of *Seminar XI*". This object is not a signifying cause, nor an imaginary cause, but a real cause. As for the phallus, it inscribed in the symbolic a lack produced by the symbolic. It is the signifier of the lack, "a peerless signifier [*signifiant sans pair*]", Lacan says, unpaired then – hence the difficulty of constructing a sexual pair with it. The object is certainly lacking, but it is not *a* lack. It is a real loss in the real. This is a first major difference. It is in the seminar *Anxiety*, two years after *Desire and its Interpretation*, that Lacan constructs it, thereby highlighting another effect of the symbolic. Lacan wanted to put this subtraction of the object *a* in relationship with the loss of life linked to reproduction by sexual means, a reproduction that makes us mortal – hence his myth of the lamella in "Position of the unconscious", writing it "*l'(a)cause première* of his desire" the way he does in "... ou pire" (Lacan, 1975a, p. 8).

There is a second difference, which is that the phallus (lowercase) was not without the father. Indeed, I won't go so far as to say that it was the son, but that it was produced from the paternal metaphor, which had been leading, and which leads straightaway to posing that in psychosis, there is a phallic failing [*carence phallique*]. Now, the decisive phallic lack, according to all of the first developments of Lacan, is that of the Other, notably represented by the mother, and whose signifier enables the child to identify his being with this lack, which separates him from identifications with the signifiers of her demand alone. This is what Lacan developed in the most explicit way concerning Schreber. Now, what about the object *a*? Does it also depend on the father?

I remind you first of all that Lacan, when asked about the question of knowing if the mathemes (S_1, S_2, $, a$) were valid in psychosis, responded in the affirmative. I think, by the way, that the question came from the previous theses on psychosis that I have just mentioned. This affirmative response means that, to Lacan's mind, the object *a*, its subtraction, was independent of phallic lack – the primordial Other as the simple locus of the signifier was enough for it to be cut out [*suffisait à sa découpe*]. Take a look at the three schemas of the division of the subject in *Anxiety*, pages 26, 114, 160 (Lacan, 2016). They aim to show how the fall of the object *a*, the subject that is divided by it, and the barred Other who is his partner [*répondant*] are, all at once, produced in a solidary fashion. Lacan's commentaries on them are not always crystal clear – in any case they are difficult to understand – but at least the writing shows beyond a shadow of a doubt, that in all three cases it is the application of A^3 (not barred) – Lacan specifies that it is the locus of the signifier, the locus of the ones [*les uns*] of the signifier then – on the S, which represents the individual before the time of the subject. It shows that it is this application that produces all at once the $, the A, and the *a* as the remainder of the operation. And here, we must not forget that A is not the partner. It is the locus of language. I quote, "that which constitutes me as unconscious", Lacan says on page 27. The base of the three schemas is written then in the same fashion:

A | S

The impact of A on the natural subject results, all at once, in $, A, *a*. Each schema positions these effects differently, but the basis of the operation is the one Lacan called "the primordial Other" in "On a question prior to any possible treatment of psychosis" – the primordial Other, he said, with which psychosis makes do. No metaphoric operation is convoked here. All that is needed is a single signifier, a unary trait of language in order to produce in solidary fashion: the bar on the subject, the bar on the Other, and the *a*. It is thus not surprising (I have developed this), that simultaneously, in this same seminar, he lays into the Freudian Oedipus, and that he ends for the first time with considerations regarding the desire of fathers, something which the metaphor did not invite. We have confirmation in

R.S.I., in the famous lesson of January 21st 1975, the one where he talks about a father and about a woman-symptom [*femme symptôme*]. Here, you will find: the Other (he writes it with a capital O) is "a matrix with two entries [*matrice à double entrée*]. The *petit a* is one of these entries." The other entry is "the one of the signifier [*l'un du signifiant*]". This is clear: the phallus was the entry for the barred Other; the object *a* is an entry for the Other, the locus of the signifier. The object *a*, *l'(a)cause* of desire is then indeed fatherless [*sans père*], unlike the phallus.

Destructivity?

What results from this desire without with the father? I am going to formulate it with an expression from Lacan found at the end of the seminar *Transference*, which is: "destructivity of desire". June 1961, it is the last page of the Seminar. I see here a first "cold shower" raining down on the idealisation of desire.

But in fact, there is in this seminar on transference, just like in most of Lacan's seminars, some non-homogenous developments that border each other, some that spring from prior elaborations – so they are reruns – and others that are more innovative. What did the prior elaborations developed in *Desire and its Interpretation* and in *The Ethics of Psychoanalysis* say about desire? Before developing this, in order to indicate the conceptual shift, I will pick out just one catchphrase from this last seminar. There, it was a question of the "tragedy of desire" – this is indeed something other than its destructivity. It is what I will show you next time.

Notes

1 [This is a play on the normal writing of "*la cause première du désir*" (the primary cause of desire). Soler explains this later on in the text.]
2 [*Je dis, moi, que le savoir affecte le corps de l'être,* […] *jusqu'à en produire les chutes dont je fais le (a), à lire objet petit* a […] *ou encore l'(a)cause première de son désir.*]
3 [A is the first letter of *Autre*, as in Other. However, in the schemas in the seminar *Anxiety*, the reader will find "A".]

Chapter IV
25th January 2014

I'll continue with the exploration of Lacan's focus on this notion of desire and linger a while on this theme in my examination of the series of the not so "human" effects of the unconscious, the very ones that generate the horror of knowledge. When we talk about the drive, its divergence regarding norms and the other is obvious. Similarly, for the symptom of jouissance, we understand immediately the necessity of regulating these jouissances in order to make them more compatible with the social link. But for desire it's more complex because if, as an effect of language, it is that which is proper to the one who speaks, it is itself a "defence against jouissance", a sort of generic defence rather than a subjective one, and so we can ask ourselves whether or not it curbs jouissance, whether or not it is a principle of humanisation. In my inquiry here, I have taken as navigational beacons the contrast between the two expressions: the "tragedy of desire" in *The Ethics of Psychoanalysis* and "the destructivity of desire" at the end of *Transference*.

Tragedy or destructivity?

The first is linked to desire conceived as a signified of the unconscious chain. In *Transference*, Lacan did not abandon this conception, and he still evokes this chain as a destiny. I give as proof of this the following sentence: "What does the analysed person come looking for in analysis?" He asks this on page 317 (Lacan, 2015). "The only thing to be found by him is, strictly speaking, the trope par excellence, the trope of tropes: what we call his fate [*destin*]." With this term trope, we cannot state more clearly the solidarity between the unconscious conceived as a chain of language and the notion of destiny. And he goes on to explain that destiny had its beginning before the subject, and he gives Antigone as an example. This is what the myth of Oedipus shows. With this, we have the idea that the unconscious desire of the subject – the desire that is latent in the chain of his unconscious, a chain which is itself inseparable from the chain of generations – the idea then that this desire supposes the operation of the father and is transmitted from the Other. To say "tragedy" is to say, is to evoke, the "it is written" of a destiny that has come from the Other, something entirely different from destructivity. It shouldn't come as a surprise then when we read in Lacan's writing that Oedipus can no longer be the main attraction [*ne peut plus tenir l'affiche*] in an era that has lost the sense of tragedy. Indeed, how could there be tragedy there where the idea of a transgenerational signifying chain that presides over the destiny of each of us is lost? This construction from the classic Lacan was coherent. However, Lacan had noticed something else, at least where sexual desire is concerned, the desire that brings bodies together.

The destructivity about which he speaks is first of all for him or her who is aimed at by desire, what we will call the desiree [*le désiré*]. Lacan establishes this concerning Alcibiades and Socrates: "the ultimate mainspring of desire", "its aim is the fall of the Other". Alcibiades's project was to "make Socrates fall off his pedestal" (Lacan, 2015, p. 176). It is what Lacan calls at one point, at the end of the seminar, the metaphor of desire as the inverse of the metaphor of love. Love is idealising. It agalmatises. And so, we can write the metaphor of love: α/a, the agalma being the idealised object a. The metaphor of desire produces, aims at, the inverse, the fall of the ideal: a/α. The inversion is clinically very perceptible in love life. Properly sexual desire goes against the founding demand for love. It promises to the partner a kind of deposition [*destitution*] and this is why being desired can generate anxiety. But destructivity is no less applicable concerning the desiring subject himself, and indeed we observe that desiring can also cause anxiety, precisely insofar as the one whom we call the subject does not have command of his desire. As a result, he is divided beyond the fact of being, moreover, abolished as an ego adapted to the norms of the world. The problem of the domestication of desire is present in every society, where it is always a question of attempting to simultaneously direct and temper it.

So, with this destructivity, what sense would there be in talking about "not giving ground relative to one's desire"? Not giving ground relative to destructivity?

The contrast with Antigone is here very instructive. Antigone does not give ground relative to the desire that tragically inscribes her in the genealogy of the Labdacides family; as a result, she certainly renounces all of her desires as a young woman – those which could be inscribed in what Lacan called the ethics of goods (the family, children, etc.) – but it is in order to feed another desire, the one that inscribes her as the daughter of the cursed family of Oedipus. This is the desire that supports the genealogical tree pinned to the father, the one from which "The Italian note" says that the analyst ought to be detached. Despite everything, by her death, Antigone immortalises her identity as the daughter of Oedipus. It is the opposite of a subjective deposition [*destitution*]. In this configuration of a destinal desire, one can say as Lacan does that "the access to desire necessitates crossing [...] not only all fear but all pity" (Lacan, 1992, p. 323) – two affects that concern the being of flesh, an opposition of the ego and of desire. And Lacan goes on to say, I quote: "There is no other good than that which may serve to pay the price for access to desire – given that desire is understood here, as we have defined it elsewhere, as the metonymy of our being. The channel in which desire is located is not simply that of the modulation of the signifying chain, but that which flows beneath it as well; that is, properly speaking, what we are as well as what we are not, our being and our non-being" (Lacan, 1992, p. 321). Considered this way, desire is the supreme value and justifies that one be able to not want to "betray his own way [*trahir sa voie*]" (Lacan, 1992, p. 321), as Lacan says when he ends the seminar *The Ethics of Psychoanalysis* with considerations about the hero and science. But how about when destiny is no more?

In this relation to desire that has come from the Other, there are only two alternatives for the subject: to identify with it as Antigone does or to curse it. And this is where Lacan calls on Sade with his cry "better not to be born", $\mu\eta$ $\varphi\nu\nu\alpha\iota$, and all the more with his wish for the second death that aspires to an annihilation not only of the being of flesh that we are but of the Other even. Don't think that this is just literature or that it is only a thing of the past. A little ten year old girl who comes to see me – who appears quite joyful, very affectionate too, and who seems only to think of playing with her girlfriends, but who suffers from love affairs that occupy her mother a little too much, and who, moreover, gets chewed out for insufficient marks at school – was telling me recently that when she was sad, she thought that she would like to die because why live, why get up, why do your homework, why go to school and come back to the house to be yelled at for bad grades ... and so, "I want to die". Then she rephrased it: no, it's not that I would like to die, in fact it's rather that "I would like to not have been born". Verbatim.

L'(a)cause première

So, once the fact has been brought to light that what generates desire is not so much the chain as it is unconscious knowledge, coming from *lalangue*, which, cutting up the body, produces in it this subtraction, those scraps [*chutes*] to which Lacan gives the name object *a*, Antigone's elation is no longer the issue.

We have to look closely at each of the successive elaborations. Desire, an effect of the signifier, is a consistent thesis in Lacan's work, from beginning to end. He first situated it as a signified. The signifier has the power to generate the signified, the signified in general – and in the signified, specifically this singular signified that is desire, desire which is neither the appetite of need, nor the demand for love. The effect of the signifier, but the signifier only operates starting with the saying of speech. It is thus in the chain of speech that we locate it, with the exception that it is not directly caused by this chain but by the signifying effect that inscribes the lack in it. It's what the phallus symbolises. Reread "The signification of the phallus", written just before "The direction of the treatment", which you should also reread.

So, how can we get a hold of it, this desire which circulates in speech as a lack caused by the signifier? "The direction of the treatment" states, "Desire must be taken literally." Yes, since it is "incompatible with speech" – carried along by it, but without being reduced to any statement [*énoncé*] whatsoever – it must be approached by means of the deciphering of letters of which speech makes use. We are thus going to track it using the play of metaphor and metonymy, which allow us to grasp that in the chain of enunciated speech, another chain is latent, is unconscious. However, the problem is only postponed: the other chain is still of the signifier. It can certainly signify desire as lack. So, with this, how can we make the link with the carnal side of desire which nevertheless imposes itself in experience?

Freud touched on this problem in situating the repressed unconscious as made of signifiers of the drive. This is what Lacan takes up in the graph of desire, which implies that the desire signified by the upper chain of the graph, the unconscious chain, is not only lack, an enigmatic lack, but a lack that is specified at the point of the jouissance of the drive. It is this articulation that his construction of the object specifies. The operation of the signifier produces, more than some subjective lack, the loss of life – here it is necessary to read, after *Anxiety*, *The Four Fundamental Concepts of Psychoanalysis*, and above all "Position of the unconscious", both produced in 1964 – the object *a*, "that which is lacking" (Lacan, 1998c, p. ix), in the form of a subtraction of life, and which is precisely *l'(a)cause première* of desire.

In summary, Lacan first articulated that desire was at the place of the signified of the unconscious chain, and also that it was the product of it, as an effect of lack, symbolised by the phallus. Then he came to think of the effect of the signifier as an effect, not of the want-to-be, but of the want-to-enjoy [*manque à jouir*], by way of the subtraction of the object *a*, cause of desire. Previously, however, before his construction of the object *a*, he had already noticed what Freud had posed from the very beginning: the joining [*articulation*] of desire founded on lack to the drive that aims at jouissance.

New problems

Some new perspectives and some new problems thus appear.

Hence the renewed problem for interpretation: how can we attain, via speech, a cause that is not of the order of language. What can be an interpretation that "bears on the object *a*"?

And then, nobody escapes this operation of subtraction, whereas psychosis had been defined by the absence of phallic signification. This is not the case with the object *a*. There is no choice here. Desire is a characteristic of the one who speaks, an effect of the S_1s of the Other, for all of the structures.

But – and here is the but – it has no specific object relative to which one would be able to not have to give ground. It is rather the contrary. The whole problem is to find for it an object that fixes it, since the cause is not the object that is aimed at. Finding an object for it is not the tragedy of desire, but only its drama. Incidentally, if Lacan said *l'(a)cause première* of desire, there ought to be a second one.[1] How can one make of an object from the world, whatever object it may be, the cause of one's desire? This is so true that at the end of *Anxiety*, he says, when speaking about the desire of the father, that "in the manifestation of his desire, the father himself knows to what *a* this desire refers". There is an inversion of the problematic: it is no longer about not giving ground relative to one's desire, it's about fixing it, even naming it. The unstable and questionable desire of the neurotic is not a desire that hesitates on its cause, but one which hesitates on the fixation of this cause by some object.

As for the destructivity of desire, if it stems from its cause, it is thus irreducible. The being of the subject divided by the signifier is reduced to this cause.

This is why the apperception of the object that he is, at the end of analysis or in other circumstances, can only be for the subject a subjective deposition [*destitution subjective*]. Consequently, the partner of desire, who holds the place of the object cause, finds himself annulled in his own being, and the subject, far from encountering the Other, encounters only himself. Remember the end of *Anxiety*, Lacan says that there is no object that is worth more than another. To the "no such thing as a sexual relationship" itself, which designates the non-relationship of the jouissances, we must add that desire makes no relationship either. Desire certainly has the power to connect, to generate interest for the other, whether this be the other subject or the other body, but no more than this. It does not stand in for the missing relationship. What does possibly stand in here is love. If you look at the schema with which Lacan, in *Encore*, completes the formulas that were presented in "L'étourdit", and which he called the formulas of sexuation, he writes that the desire of the man is steered in the direction of the woman partner [*la partenaire*], but it aims at the object *a*. Reciprocally, the part of the desire of the barred Woman, which is steered in the direction of the man, aims at the phallus – in both cases then, at a little something that is not the partner. Suffice it to say that it is not enough for a desire to be hetero-sexual for it to lose its destructivity.

$$\begin{array}{c} \cancel{S} \longrightarrow | \longrightarrow a \\ \Phi \longleftarrow | \longrightarrow \text{LaF} \end{array}$$

As a result, a new problem arises: on what conditions can a desire fix itself in such a way that its possible subjective and/or social destructivity be either counterbalanced or contained? And this is the whole problem of humanisation … the humanisation of desire. And Lacan yet convokes, at the end of *Anxiety*, the father as the one who offers "the question of the concept of anxiety a real guarantee" (Lacan, 2016, p. 338). So, is the father necessary here? That's the major question of humanisation. Without the Freudian Oedipus, is humanisation in peril?

In any case, desire is indeed this "black god", which must not be confused "with the curly-haired sheep of the good shepherd", as Lacan pricelessly says in order to make fun of the followers of genital oblativity. The French current of psychoanalysis, which developed this theme of genital oblativity that is supposed to emerge at the end of analysis, was dreaming, obviously, of substituting the gift for destructivity. Which just goes to show that the horror of knowledge is an empty expression. In any case, desire, if you have followed me, is not so humanising as one might have believed with the first developments of Lacan. It is most likely not tragic, but worse – it is senseless and destructive.

The agalma of desire

How is it possible, as I have said before, that with all of this, we have made an analytic value out of desire? We should, at least in psychoanalysis, manage to talk about desire, and even of the desire of the analyst, without idealisation. Instead, the opposite is the case. This is quite obvious. If you have any doubts about it, read the preludes to next July's international meeting on "The paradoxes of desire", and you will see that they don't all avoid the pitfall I am talking about. Sometimes they even make a lyricism out of it. It's comical, and I wonder about it. This idealisation is perfectly suspect, analytically speaking, because like every idealisation, it works against the real. It is even a defence against the real, and what is in question is the real of desire, not desire as a simple signified. How can we have idealised desire if we have grasped what Lacan calls its destructivity?

It is first of all certain that desiring is in itself a satisfaction. It is one of the paradoxes in question since in desire, we are deprived of that which we desire, and yet there is satisfaction all the same. This is because desire, the experience of desire, generates the feeling of living much more than possession does. The pain of depression which suspends the vector of desire is a negative proof of it. Ernest Jones, the biographer of Freud, had moreover proposed the notion of *aphanisis*, which, according to him, was a fear of and a suffering from not desiring, something which he identified in neurotics. Indeed, the analyst receives this complaint from the subjects in whom desire is still undecided, which quite often translates into a feeling of vacuousness and indecision, as if here there were a desire for desiring. At bottom, we can make the relationship of desire to life much clearer. Jouissance as a phenomenon of the body supposes the life of the body, of this "fitted out" body [*corps appareillé*] that language, for that matter, mortifies. But desire, which supposes precisely this negativising effect of language that Lacan presented in different forms, is that which gives life, not to the body, but to the subject, in the sense that this is what animates the subject; this has nothing to do then with the life of the organism as such.

Moreover, it is a fact – there is nothing in the animal resembling anything like a desire. There is only the rhythms of need and of a satiety that is transitorily possible. Desire is what remains of the appetency of need in a being whose needs are alienated in the Other from the fact of their submission to the demand as articulated, what remains unappeasable. Hence its eccentric side in the double sense of the term: coming from the other scene, and as a result – I am quoting Lacan here – the "paradoxical, deviant, erratic, eccentric, and even scandalous nature of desire that distinguishes it from need" (Lacan, [1958b] 2006, p. 579). The paradox of desire is quite noticeable, clinically, in the fact that, on the one hand there is a satisfaction of desiring – one feels dynamic, alive – and on the other, there is a fear of desiring, even more, an anxiety of desire [*angoisse du désir*]. The entire seminar *Anxiety* is given in order to say that anxiety pertains to desire as desire of the Other.

This contrast is precisely what makes the notion of unsatisfied desire – which we make a big deal about, notably concerning hysteria – quite problematic because unsatisfied desire is essentially desire itself, whereas, we have realised for a long time now that a satisfied desire was just as problematic because, when it occurs, fulfilled desire is a desire that is snuffed out. In fact, if we attempt a phenomenology of desires, we see that the configurations are diverse. There is first of all what I am going to call the transitive desires, by analogy with transitive demands, which

Lacan uses. I mean by this, desire specified by an object, the object at which it aims: desire for gadgets, desire for a woman, desire for a man, desire to have a child – ah, the desire to have a child nowadays. In this case, desire is experienced as deprivation, and in a rather painful mode. This is already something different when desire aims at the realisation of some undertaking. In this case, in the time that it takes, hope and action give desire its dynamic, rather positive, colouring. But Lacan's analyses of desire do not concern so much desires in the plural, but desire in the singular, even if the routes by which it is realised pass by multiple realities.

The paradoxes of desire, in the singular – unconscious desire, Freud called it, because we do not know what it aims at – all arise from the difference, from the gap, that there is between desire's cause and its object, and therefore, between being the cause or being the object of desire. When desire is reduced to its cause – as is the case in hysteria, whose identification "bears on desire, that is to say, on the lack taken as object, and not on the cause of the lack" (Lacan, 1975b, p. 15) – one then enjoys [*jouit de*] the dissatisfaction of desire … the dissatisfaction of the desire of the Other [*de l'Autre*]. As for the object of desire – but here we have to use the plural – the objects of desire, can we be satisfied by them? Yes, and no, given that no object whatsoever *is* the cause of desire. Contrary to the various adages that are whispered to us, it is because we have found something, but found something else, that we keep on searching (when I speak of adage, I think first of all about the one that was going around about God: "you wouldn't be looking for me if you hadn't already found me", which means that in order to look for him, it is already necessary to perceive that I am lacking him. And then the one from Picasso, about which Lacan makes a point: "I don't search, I find." That makes sense for Picasso, but we should point out to him that he does not find so long as he is deterred from continuing to search). There are indeed *eurekas* of desire, but they are always ephemeral because the surplus jouissances obtained [*plus-de-jouir obtenus*] do not suspend the lost cause that stimulates again and again.

Note

1 [There is sort of a play on words here that is derived from a possible meaning of *première*, which can mean not only "main" or "primary", but also "first" or "original."]

Chapter V

29th January 2014

I tried to show that the question of a regulation is posed not only for jouissance, but also for desire. When I say "regulation", this does not indicate that there exists some possible agent of this regulation. It is a question about the apparatuses [*appareils*] that are at work. It is not enough to give as an answer to this question: language. Because, of course, it (language) determines desire, the jouissance of the drive, and symptom jouissance, but on top of this, an additional regulation is called for, which would be, let us say, a socialising regulation.

In fact, I am insisting on this point concerning desire because, when it comes to the symptom of jouissance, with its traits of perversion, language is indeed its apparatus, but it is fixed in a contingent way, with a contingency that tips over into a necessity, which no longer ceases to be written [*ne cesse plus de s'écrire*], and so it is not domesticable. The same goes for the drives, being effects of language, of course, but which are dissident by nature. Desire is different, and this is what the word "dialectic" indicates in "dialectic of desire". This is what I will take, then, as my point of departure.

If the object, being an effect of language, is *l'(a)cause première* of desire, we can ask ourselves about all of the various desires. I talked about fixed desire, and I'm now going to correct this because it's rather jouissance that is fixed. Lacan says "finite" desires. We could also employ the term "determination" and ask: what makes it possible to determine desire's lack whose cause alone does not decide? What makes it possible to orient its vector towards a goal that is not only specific but stable?

When we talk about types of desire, like questionable or decided desire, or pure desire and desire that is not pure, or crazy desires to which Lacan alludes in *The Four Fundamental Concepts of Desire*, or specified desires, like the desire of the analyst – in all of these cases, we are talking about desires that are "determined" in the double meaning of the word: they don't vacillate, and they have a specific aim. I say aim rather than object because the determination of a desire is not made by the expected surplus jouissance alone. Its symbolic and imaginary coordinates are always more complex. It is at the level of this determination that the question of the humanisation of desire is posed.

What contributes – in the capacity of a second cause then if the object *a* is the first cause [*la cause premiere*] – to giving to desire its determined forms?

The trait that characterises them, phenomenologically, is constancy, just like with the drives. We have several answers in Lacan's teaching concerning the factors, which, owing to the fact of the unconscious, can contribute to this determination of a desire: first of all, the fantasy, and this isn't new with Lacan, but was already in Freud; the paternal function, of course, is also involved, and we will see how; the discourses, each one of them determining both some types of desire and some types of jouissance; and then at the end, the Borromean knot, without which, "a desire is not conceivable" (Lacan, 1974–1975, lesson of April 15th 1975), Lacan says in *R.S.I.* It will thus be necessary to update this question of desire using the final elaborations of Jacques Lacan.

Types of desires

We sometimes speak of "decided" desire. The notion is in vogue among Lacanians, and all the more so as it is precisely the opposite of the neurotic's desire. What is it? A desire specified by its objective, which doesn't vacillate, and which even often takes precedence over all things, and which thus spares nothing. It is at this level that its possible destructivity is situated. We see the effects of it on lineage when a father or a mother are, for example, a man or woman of vocation, whatever the vocation may be. All of the desires that preside over what we call a vocation – there where these vocations exist, in the field of art probably, and also in the field of science – are "decided" desires. In those cases, desire becomes something close to what we call a passion, and which doesn't always get very good press, in the field of philosophy anyways.

Does a "decided" desire have a meaning at the sexual level? The desire for a given partner, a specific partner, can be maintained over time – it happens – but we wouldn't qualify it as "decided" desire, even if it is stable. We will say, on the contrary, "he or she is bitten", an expression whose connotations exclude any decision whatsoever. In our language, as soon as we say "decided" desire, it is like when we say about a person that he or she is "decided", this connotes constancy and somewhat resembles an ego-level will [*volonté moïque*]. As for those whom the sexual thing captivates in a decided manner, independently of the objects, we qualify them as "excited", even "obsessed", rather than as "decided", which poses in both cases, the question of what is behind the principle of their constancy.

In any case, a "decided" desire is a finite desire, the contrary of a pure desire. A pure desire is a desire impelled by the lack of the object *a*, but with an objectal specification. As for pure desire, Lacan evokes Spinoza: a desire that consists in fitting in with the signifying order of the universe, an order that is supposed to be identical to God himself, a singular desire then, which elides the singularity of the one who desires in order to integrate him into the universal order. It is clearly distinguished from the moral law of Immanuel Kant, which is supposed to unconditionally animate all of my maxims. This law only takes on its rigour as a law, a law which does not vacillate, from the fact that it excludes every consideration of any pathological object, whatever it may be, pathology designating in Kant not the anomaly but the objects that are not derived from reason, the objects of sensibility, that is to say, all of the objects of attachment or of desire, all of the objects of the human affection. Except that Lacan, in writing "Kant with Sade", proposes an interpretation of Kantian morality, which decidedly, and unwittingly, falls within the jurisdiction of the Sadean fantasy.

What does the analyst want?

Among the "decided" desires, there is one that interests us in particular: the desire of the analyst, the one we make a big deal about, but it would be better not to heroise it. Lacan says that it is not a pure desire, precisely because it has a specific aim, a set objective, which is the "absolute difference" (Lacan, 1998d, p. 276) of the analysand. Absolute difference, the expression appears contradictory, but it can be easily defined. The signifier is defined by its differential structure. From the phoneme, up to the whole of discourse, it is only identified in differentiating itself from another signifier. Thus, it is always relative. By definition, a difference implies a relation to another term, and thus a relativity. Absolute difference, on the contrary, is a difference that is identified without any comparison. When Lacan says that it enters into play when the subject is inscribed for the first time under the "primordial signifier", this means that the "primordial signifier" is not a signifier among others and so is not differential. It is the index of an experience: either the unary trait of a trauma – and this is the first definition of the symptom in "The instance of the letter in the unconscious" – or a signifier that has become a letter, an enjoyed letter [*lettre jouie*], identical to itself, without a referent. Said otherwise, it is identified by jouissance, which whatever it may be, whatever its intensity may be, traumatic or not, is unparalleled, unique, singular. We find the same expression again, sixteen years later when Lacan talks about the "analysed" as "scattered, ill-matched individuals [*épars désassortis*]" (Lacan, 1998c, p. ix). Singularity, which is not particularity, is the word from common language that most approaches the sense of the term "absolute difference". Suffice it to say that absolute difference does not come from the Other but, on the contrary, effects a separation from the Other. It falls under the category of "*Y a d'l'Un*".[1] The "*Y a d'l'Un*" can be commented on in various ways: in connection with the primordial signifier, if you want, but also in connection with the One [*Un*] of the Borromean Knot, but in every case, it is excepted from the ones [*uns*] that are, amongst other things, differential. Absolute difference, and the "decided" desire that aims at it, are limits, breaking points of the dialectic of desire. Because the term "dialectic" indicates the contrary, the relation to the Other and the potential fluctuations that this relation makes possible.

It is because desire is in part dialectical that a desire of the analyst can be produced in an analysis, can be the product of the analytic operation independently of the anterior predispositions of the subject. Analysis supposes and proves that a desire can be transformed, that a new desire can be brought into focus. And how? By the operation … am I going to say … of speech? No, speech is not enough, neither the one that is emitted, nor the one that is listened to. Starting in the 1970s, specifically beginning with the seminar on the "Analytic act", Lacan poked fun at listening [*l'écoute*]. This is because the act does not consist in listening. It does not look to interpret speech, to interpret what is said. It aims at the cause of desire. A new desire can be procured by the operation ... of the analytic act. And this new desire is a changing of the subject, not of his symptoms, even if there are therapeutic effects.

$$a \longrightarrow \mathcal{S}$$

As an aside, this efficacy of the act is due to its policy [*politique*], that is to say, to its goal – this leaves in suspense the question of its means. This efficacy of the act in a psychoanalysis is possibly what founds at once the worries about and the hatreds for psychoanalysis. Worry about possible manipulation, and hatred when "the new" is not produced. This, at least, is my interpretation of the hatred for psychoanalysis. I am coming from the idea that it is among people who have gone through psychoanalysis that this hatred is the most virulent. I think it is because they do not get over not having been renewed by it. And so, they write "black books [*livres noirs*]",[2] because they think they have been the victim of a false promise. This is because when analysis fails to satisfy the subject, there are two possible subjective roads for him to take: either he supposes that this is because of him, and he assumes it as his limitation, or he supposes that it is because of the method, or because of the analyst that he had. Confronted with this, the psychoanalyst can do nothing, and this is why contrary to what Freud hoped for, the act is perhaps subversive, but it is not the plague.

What is certain is that the analyst wants something concerning the other, his analysand, and that he is tasked with bringing this wanting to bear [*faire passer à l'acte ce vouloir*]. It is at this same juncture that the question of scoundrels [*canailles*] is introduced into psychoanalysis and it is not by accident if Lacan talks about it explicitly. According to his definition, anyone who wants to be the Other for someone, or for someones, is a scoundrel. I mean by this, he who wants to decide someone's desire [*décider du désir de quelqu'un*]. We must not, then, confuse the scoundrel with thugs, with bandits, etc. Scoundrels are among respectable figures. So, scoundrelism [*canaillerie*], a noun that is feminine in French, threatens every educator, from simple parents to professionals of all kinds, and they escape it only by their failure. The fact that desire is dialectical, and thus subject to variations, does not actually imply that it can be controlled. Educating is an impossibility because the Other himself is not the master of his desire. The result: education certainly operates, but it is impossible to account for the desire that operates therein, and thus to foretell its effects. Lacan applies this thesis to Sade's endeavours to educate virtue. The scoundrel is thus not the master, who certainly operates, but based on a master signifier, and he has no concern about the desire of the slave. Neither is the scoundrel a cynic who has no other cause but himself, I mean, his own jouissance. Nor is he a hysteric, who wants, certainly, to make the Other desire, but who aims not at the determination of desire but at its opposite. As for the analyst, he aims at an effect on the desire of the analysand, different from the effect aimed at by the scoundrel. We can write this opposition:

For the scoundrel: $A \longrightarrow \$$;
For the analyst: $a \longrightarrow \$$.

The analyst orients the cure, but he knows, has to know, that desire is already oriented and that it is a question of revealing what orients it. Lacan said that one has to deny analysis to scoundrels. The problem is that one doesn't know in advance who is a scoundrel, who has inherited a scoundrel's desire – because Lacan thinks that it is inherited. Why does one have to refuse them analysis? Because, in such a situation, if the analysis hasn't cured his scoundrelism, this puts a scoundrel in the position of analyst. There are more of these than you might think. Lacan pointed them out within the IPA, but there are others. What they do best is to fail in the directing of desire. Or else the analysis will have cured him of his scoundrelism, but he will have become stupid because of it. How should we take this? When Lacan talks about stupidity, let's remember his thesis: the signifier is stupid, and during the course of analysis, one says stupid things, that is to say signifiers, without caring about their meaning. Once analysed, a scoundrel will then have learned that as stupid as it is, it's the signifier that leads us, the unconscious signifiers that object to anyone being the agent of desire. And so, he will probably be stupid enough to rely only on the sole play of signifiers, via free association, and so he will forget the other cause, that of the object ... cause, and that of the saying [*dire*]. Said otherwise, accepting his impotence, he will no longer believe in the efficacy of the act, and maybe he will be delighted with his own listening, like those of whom Lacan spoke in the "Compte rendu de l'acte".

I mentioned the destructivity of desire, but we must realise the degree of this destructivity. Lacan introduced it concerning the amorous couple, but not concerning all of the forms of desire. It is the drive, with its quest for surplus jouissance [*plus-de-jouir*], implicated in sexual desire, which makes destructivity out of desire. Even for sexual desire, it doesn't always go to extremes – for example, the case of this Japanese man who was all over the news for killing a woman before eating her piece by piece – but in the best of cases, as I have already said, desire reduces the partner to the object *a*, the rib of which Adam was deprived, according to Genesis. Next to sexual desire, there is another desire where the question of destructivity is raised: the desire for a child. The child, too, is called forth as object. This is in some ways an *a priori* deposition [*destitution*], the whole problem being precisely one of knowing how in each case the child will be able to emerge from this alienation. Nevertheless, all desires are not so destructive of the other. The paradox of the desire of the analyst is that he aims, on the contrary, to establish [*instituer*] the other to whom he is devoted, that is, the analysand, but – and here is the paradox – to establish him in revealing to him, either what there is of something that is structurally deposing [*destituant*], or else the object *a* if we take the formulas of "La proposition", or the unarity of jouissance if we take the later formulas. In this sense, this is a fact, the desire of the analyst is intrinsically tied to the desire to know.

The well-known "subjective deposition [*destitution subjective*]" that is necessary to make an analyst according to "La proposition de 1967" is a gain of knowledge, incidentally. It consists for the subject in apprehending his equivalence, the equivalence of all of his elaborations of language to the object *a* – the object, which, not being represented by any signifier whatsoever, is not, however, any the less imaginarised in the construction of the fantasy. *Sicut palea*, said Saint Thomas, who was often quoted by Lacan. In 1967, this deposition appeared necessary to Lacan for a subject to be capable of holding, in practice, the place of the object *a*, cause of the analysand.

The notion of the analytic act, put forth just after this "proposition", is coherent with this construction because in the act, as Lacan says, it is "the object that (is active), and the subject [who is] subverted" (Lacan, 1968, p. 34). One might believe with this that the analytic act de-subjectivises the desire of the analyst, even replaces it. But this would be the opposite meaning because the desire of the analyst is the condition, the support of the possible act. The "active object" means active cause of desire. Here is the formula that I propose to you for the desire of the analyst: it is the subject supposed to the analytic act, not the subject supposed to know, even if this act implicates the desire of the analyst. But – and this is a paradox – this act itself is demonstrated only by its effects, and it is alone in proving that there is *some* [*du*] psychoanalyst, emphasising the *some*, as Lacan does. This *some* implies two things: first of all, we cannot name, in a credible way, *a* psychoanalyst, a psychoanalyst's desire, but then, there is *some* [*du*] psychoanalyst only on the condition that there not be only one. So, not one (not a single one), but not only one. This formula carries the necessity of a School with its pass.

Since psychoanalysis is a practice that, as Lacan says, recognises in desire the truth of the subject (Lacan, [1963] 2006), becoming an analyst is a changing of the subject. Last time, I cited this passage from the seminar *Transference* where Lacan says that desire is the being of the subject, his being of not-being [*son être de non étant*]. Then comes the moment where, in a shift, Lacan says that the being of the subject is the object *a*, let us say, his being without essence, since it is the object without predicate, a-predictive. But in both cases, it is the subject who is concerned, not his symptoms, because they are phenomena of the body, of the body that the subject has. With this you understand that it is ludicrous to ask oneself, as some do, whether Lacan, in the end, didn't elide, even do away with his reference to desire in favour of jouissance. To do away with the reference to desire would be to do away with the reference to the subject, whereas the notion of speaking-being [*parlêtre*] does not eliminate that of the subject. In putting the object *a* cause of desire at the heart of the Borromean knot, he even makes of it, implicitly, a central, un-eliminable reference. And even when he pronounces, "There's something-of-a-One [*Y a d'l'Un*]", in 1971, of a Unarity, in 1977, it is a question of a nodal unarity, the unarity of what he names in *R.S.I.* the "real subject" that I sometimes call the Borromean subject – so, this One [*Un*] is a knot. He knots a desire to imaginary representations and to jouissances inscribed in the knot, phallic jouissance and the jouissance of meaning [*jouissance du sens*], because, he says it, the object determines the various jouissances, whatever they may be.

All this to say, once more, that the desire of the analyst, which certainly has an efficacy, is no more nameable than the object *a*. And it is this, possibly, which pushes towards idealisation, which I wonder about, and even towards mystification. Lacan says at the end of the *Écrits:* analysis is not the science of the object. In *Le Sinthome*, he indicates that analysis is not a religion of the object *a* either. I quote: "We don't believe in the object, we observe desire, and we put forward the object as the objectivised cause." In other words, we do not believe in the object as one would believe in God.

I conclude from this, and I invite you to conclude with me, that we have not really heard Lacan's development when we idealise desire. Desire, for he who speaks, is not, in the first place, a choice, but a destiny, which means a structural effect. Desiring is thus not a performance. What one idealises, in fact, is never desire as such, but always a determined desire, and for example, the desire of the analyst. But in doing this, when one idealises it, one opens, without knowing it possibly, the chapter on the competition of desires. I would willingly add to the racism of jouissances – which Lacan talks about and which finds its source in the various discourses – the competition of desires, the competition of tastes in matters of desire, which is competition of the various truths that the various discourses harbour.

Up to what point does logic command?

However, Lacan's thesis, at least in 1967, in the "Compte rendu de la logique du fantasme", was that there where the act is, it is logic that commands. Desire is supposed to the act, gives it its aim, but the pathways of the act, the guide of the act, is not the desire of the analyst, it is the logic of discourse. The ethics [*éthique*] of the act is not "*éthiquette*", Lacan says. Thus, it is not a respect for the rules, and he puts the "h" of ethics in etiquette in order to indicate that adhering to etiquette – in other words, following certain standards in psychoanalysis – is a choice. And so, in the ethics of the act, "logic commands", "unless", he says, "some types, some norms, are added to it". But "the psychoanalytic act [...] ought not get mixed up in this". Note the nuance of a kind of shady business that there is in the term "mixed up". With the act, it is thus not a question of a norm. It is a question of following what the logic of language and of discourse imposes as impossible or necessary. The act does not choose its own pathways. It follows the lines of structure.

Let me pause for a moment on the function of logic in psychoanalysis. Lacan had recourse to it, and he defended this choice, notably in "L'étourdit" and well before it as a matter of fact. I quote: "Resorting to the not-all [*pas-tout*], to *l'hommoinsun*,[3] that is, to the impasses of logic, is, in showing the way out of the fictions of social life, to make another *fixion* of the real: that is, of the impossible which fixes it from the structure of language" (Lacan, 1973, p. 35).[4] The orientation towards the real that Lacan gave to psychoanalysis thus passes, at least at first, through logic – here, the logic of sets. Lacan resorts to this because, in the handling of language, only the impossible acts as a blocker of the real [*fait butée de réel*], and the impossible, unlike impotence, is logically demonstrated. Hence the oft repeated thesis: the real is the impossible. However, the discourse of logic, as much as that of mathematics, whichever one it may be, from Euclid to Cantor, this discourse is purely formal, thus empty, made of letters and procedures that do not signify anything. It is the discourse "most void of meaning" (Lacan, 1973, p. 34) that there is. Lacan gives as a reminder in "L'étourdit", the remarks of Bertrand Russell addressing the embarrassment that mathematics has with its language because it does not know what it is talking about (Lacan, 1973, p. 23). In the same way, for psychoanalysis, two logics are in play, that of the language-unconscious and that of discourse, which implies the difference between the saying [*dire*] and the saids [*dits*]. We often repeat that logic is the science of the real and Lacan formulated it as such, but he drew a line at the beginning of "L'étourdit". I quote. It is through logic that analytic discourse "touches the real, in the encountering of it as impossible, which is why it is this discourse (the analytic one) that carries it (logic) to its ultimate power: science, I have said, of the real". Logic becomes the science of the real through psychoanalysis. In other words, in order for logic, which does not know what it is talking about, to become the science of the real, it needs a boost [*appoint*]. The discourse of psychoanalysis brings to it a language of the unconscious, which is not void of meaning because it is the language of jouissance that speaks. "Without jouissance, all that is necessary is mathematical logic in order to make superstition of scepticism" (Lacan, 1970, p. 79), as is said in "Radiophonie"; and in "L'étourdit", Lacan clarifies that the "logical power" of the not-all "is inhabited by feminine jouissance [*s'habite de la jouissance féminine*]". Obviously, with this reference to jouissance, he implicitly introduces another real, the one of what is living [*du vivant*], which is necessary in order to enjoy [*jouir*], a material in thirds [*une matière en tiers*], which he will inscribe in the Borromean knot. As a result, when we talk about the not-all, it is necessary to clearly distinguish its logic, which goes way beyond the question of women and which gives it flesh. We will see whether the commentaries on the seminar *Encore* in the soirées of our school will be up to the task presented by this logic of the not-all, or whether these commentaries will remain fascinated by what can inhabit this logic. I insist on this point so that we not be mistaken about the analyst: the fact that he falls within the scope of [*relève de*] the logic of the not-all, as Lacan stated it, does not signify that he shares what is called the other jouissance, as we have heard in the past, with the idea of a feminisation at the end of analysis, of the production of a new mystic. We no longer hear this anymore, which is good. In any case for him [the analyst], contrary to how it is for woman [*la femme*], and because he presides over a discursive order, we can respond to the question of what he wants.

Let me go back to the act (which I only evoked in relation to desire), the act without norms then – or perhaps. This is a question that I pose to "L'étourdit". When Lacan says, on page 12 of "L'étourdit", after having set out the difference between the saying [*dire*] and the said [*dit*] implied in every actual discourse and after having affirmed the saying [*dire*] of Freud "there is no such thing as a sexual relationship" – from this, I quote, "we must obtain two halves which do not get confused in their *coïtération*". These are obviously the two halves of the heterosexual couple. Is this not a norm? Why do we need these two hetero halves? The current debates on homosexuality specifically denounce a social norm on this point. It is indeed difficult to think that it is logic that demands these two halves. Lacan clarifies: half means that it is a matter of the ego, and the ego implies the norms of civil status and of anatomy, thus of the imaginary, but not only. Half implies sexed identifications that engage the phallus and thus the symbolic, which can indeed sketch two parts, whether being or having the phallus – it can, but why is it necessary?

Is it only to give an account for what is a fact, namely that there are heterosexual couples, and that it is a question of explaining how they are possible despite the non-relationship? Possibly. It's what Freud did with his Oedipus. However, the text evokes a necessity that would require finding two halves, and which is not the symbolic one, of the phallus, but the real one, of actual reproduction. He asks: how does man, who has an unconscious, and thus no [sexual] relationship, reproduce? At this level of the question, the two halves are not those of eroticism, but of reproduction. A question then: why is it necessary to reproduce? It is because, failing reproduction, everything could indeed be resolved demographically – meaning the disappearance of the species. This theme permeates the text. Life reproduces, certainly, but what is necessary so that the one who speaks reproduces? That the species ought to survive, is this not a norm? We talk a lot these days about the disappearance of species. Would this not be the displacement of a worry concerning our species? In fact, for a little while now, we have begun inviting in the field of culture, on the radio, in the press, the voice of the demographers. This astonishes me. It was not the case thirty years ago. We invite them obviously for the economic repercussions of demography, but on the horizon, there are repercussions of survival. After the dissolution of his school, in the letter of March 11th 1980, entitled "D'écolage",[5] Lacan attributes to Freud "a reduction of the genital to the fact of reproduction". This is effectively what Freud does when he poses that the genital phase is distinguishable from the phallic phase because reproduction is possible. Lacan does not reduce the genital to reproduction – he is not from the same era. Nevertheless, the necessity of the two halves is inseparable from the necessities supposed for reproduction, and it is not logic that creates this necessity. Here, something like a desire to survive is necessary, which is obviously undeducible, and even undecidable. Ultimately, it seems to me that what Freud was aiming at, obscurely, with his life drives and death drives, beyond the problem of individual subjective problems, haunts this logic of "L'étourdit." No doubt about it, the regulation of desires and the regulation of jouissance involve more than social links, even more than the couples of love – beyond this, they engage the real of life, the survival of the species. Not so sure that with our science we can count on the fictional future to ensure mass reproduction, without passing through hetero-sexuality.

Notes

1 [Although his phrase is virtually untranslatable, we could perhaps propose the following: "There's something-of-a-One."]
2 [Here, *livres noirs* most likely refers to the book, *Le Livre Noir de la Psychanalyse*.]
3 [This is an alternative writing of *au moins un* [at least one], but here Lacan replaces *au* with *homme* [man]].
4 ["*Recourir au* pastout, à l'hommoinsun, *soit aux impasses de la logique, c'est, à montrer l'issue hors des fictions de la Mondanité, faire* fixion *autre du réel: soit de l'impossible qui le fixe de la structure de langage.*"]
5 [This is first of all a play on the word *décollage* which means "taking off", for example, in an airplane. Here *d'écolage*, a neologism, makes use of the word *école* (school) to create a pun indicating a "taking off" from the school.]

Chapter VI

12th February 2014

I am going to transition into what is, in fact, my question for the year, that of the function of the father in this regulation, said to be a humanising regulation of desires and jouissances. The question that I chose leads straight to it, from Freud, and it is an opportunity for me to come back to it.

We know Freud's first answer. For him this function of the father is crucial. It is what he elaborates under the term of Oedipus in the general sense, by which he attempts to conceive the establishment of the law at once in civilisation, with *Totem and Taboo*, and in each subjectivity, with what Lacan named the "*historiole*"[1] of Oedipus. This law is supposed to introduce both limitation and order in the relations between the sexes and generations because it must not be forgotten that the couple of jouissance is also the couple of reproduction. In the myth, limitation is stated in terms of "not all of the women", and order is given by specific exclusions of certain women amongst them, which vary, incidentally, according to each culture, but they are present in all of them. Maurice Godelier reminded us of this recently in the school.

We know Lacan's formulas regarding this Oedipus. They reject it, and here, the whole of Lacan's position with respect to Freud is involved. I insist regularly on the Freudian anchoring of Lacan's developments. Nevertheless, with his advancements, Lacan entered into a critique of the limits of Freudian psychoanalysis, from the point at which Freud left it.

A few references on this subject. Lacan even claims to pass, I quote, "to the other side of psychoanalysis insofar as it is the discourse of Freud, him being suspended". Analytic discourse, such as he writes it, which puts the object a in the place of the semblant[2] would thus be the other side of psychoanalysis as Freud's discourse. Additionally, this passage functions, he says, "without recourse to the Name-of-the-Father, from which, I have said, I am abstaining" (Lacan, 1970, p. 81). He says it at the moment when he has just constructed the structure of the discourses. This other side thus means that psychoanalysis, at the point where Freud left it, is written with the master's discourse, which gives it a master signifier in the place of the semblant.[3]

Indeed, the practice of Freud is free association in which he deciphers signifiers of the unconscious, S_2s, producing the object a as surplus jouissance [*plus-de-jouir*], this being why Lacan can say that the analysand consumes [*consomme*] jouissance. That Freud held himself to this practice illuminates the impasse of the ends of analysis to which he bore witness and which he recognised with wonderful honesty, if you think of it.

I can also evoke the end of the Proposition of 1967 where Lacan returns to what he calls the oedipal ideology. I will come back to this.

As for the "Italian note", it persists in this critique, in a drastic way. Having talked about Freud's love affairs with truth, he adds: "It is the model from which the analyst, if there are any, represents the fall." Suffice it to say, as he formulates it later in *Le Sinthome*, that it is psychoanalysis itself which – I am still quoting – "in succeeding, proves that we can just as well do without the Name-of-the-Father". I'll leave for the moment the rest of the sentence in suspense (Lacan, 2005, p. 316).

As a result, the expression "beyond Oedipus [*au-delà de l'Œdipe*]" has become in our circle a sort of *logion*, or fixed expression, which is transmitted from mouth to mouth concerning the teaching of Lacan without one always knowing what it really conveys. There are many such expressions: "there is no such thing as a sexual relationship", "a woman is a symptom", "to love is to give what you don't have", etc. It is Barbara Cassin who talked about the *logions* of Lacan, and rightly so I think, and done positively, to designate expressions, fixed sayings, which are striking and which are transmitted, and whose significations vary according to the different readings of it. But Lacan, more ironically negative, talked about "pretty fossils" (Lacan, 1974–1975, lesson of April 15th 1975) in order to stigmatise, concerning the diverse and multiple formulas that he had produced, a literal transmission, although not algebraic, so automatic and repetitive that it drains them of their meaning [*sens*]. This is not a problem in culture, but for psychoanalysis it is a problem, because without their meaning, how could they contribute to orienting analysts in their daily practice? And so, I mean to follow the steps of Lacan and above all, above all, to see how far he went.

I am not so sure, at the point at which I am engaging it, what exactly Lacan's point of arrival is. Sometimes, I have asked myself, in reading and on many occasions, if he himself isn't sometimes backing away from the unprecedented character of what he had just put forward. I'll take an example: what he calls the bourgeois family, the conjugal one. There is praise for it in *Les complexes familiaux*, in opposition to communitarian child-rearing [*éducations communautaires*] (1938); in 1958, he sees in the family the irreducible cell of civilisation, the "final residue" of the fragmentation of links; in 1967, in "La proposition sur le psychanalyste de l'École", it is more ambiguous: concerning the Oedipus complex he says that it is necessary to relativise it, but also to restore its radicalness, and concerning the family, he highlights that oedipal ideology exempted sociology from taking sides on "the value of the family, of the existing family, of the petit bourgeois family in the civilisation of science", without one knowing if he affirms this value or not.

He wanted to make a French garden of the Oedipus complex, certainly, but if he did so, in any case, he did not succeed in passing it on. This French garden is the expression by which he qualified his return to Freud. This consisted in introducing something like a "highway [*grand route*]" into Freud's tiny and multiple intricate paths, which are very often paths "that lead nowhere", after Heidegger's expression. Especially concerning the Oedipus complex, Lacan energetically denounced the Freudian confusion. In "L'étourdit", he stigmatises the Oedipus complex as a "parasitic organism" grafted onto the saying [*dire*] of Freud, the "There is no such thing as a sexual relationship", and he adds:

> It is no small affair for a female cat to find here its young and the reader, a meaning.
> The mess is insurmountable concerning what of castration is pinned down here, concerning the defiles whereby love intermingles with incest, concerning the function of the father, concerning the myth where Oedipus is redoubled by the comedy of the *Père-Orang* [Father-Orang, or Father-orating], of the *pérorant Outang* [perorating utang].
>
> (Lacan, 1973, p. 13)

And here is what seems to me a good reason for examining what Lacan brought, in terms of understanding [*de lumière*] and rationality, with his successive definitions of the father and his a-spherical topology recusing the whole of the universe, and then with his Borromean knot and its possible *suppléances*.

The highway of the metaphor[4]

I'll begin with the beginning, the paternal metaphor, which is the most well-known, and which, it is certain, has not been relegated to the past for everyone.

I'll first lay out the major steps in order to anticipate the itinerary.

However, reread in the *après-coup* of what comes next, these oedipal developments appear as very surprising but nevertheless indicate to us Lacan's true point of departure.

The next step, quite well-known, is the single lesson of what was supposed to be a year of seminar entitled *The Names-of-the-Father*, for which he substituted *The Four Fundamental Concepts of Psychoanalysis*. This is November 1963 and it is thus contemporary with his "excommunication" from the association founded by Freud. Then comes "L'étourdit", in July 1972, after "... ou pire". A complex text if there ever was one, and whose significance concerning our theme will have to be determined. And finally, the introduction of the father who names, of the father of the name, which inverts the expression the Name-of-the-Father, the father *Sinthome*. No detour on this journey – but rather the rolling out of a time for understanding and of the logic that presides over it.

The metaphor was the Oedipus complex shaped into a French garden. He writes it in "On a question prior to any possible treatment of psychosis", drafted between December 1957 and January 1958, – the dates are important – and we have to add all of the texts of the seminars around it. Those that precede: *La Relation d'Objet* and the one on *The Psychoses*. But also, the one that is contemporary to it, *Les formations de l'inconscient*, 1957–1958. In this seminar, the first trimester is consecrated to the witticism, but on January 8th, while he is finishing drafting "On a question prior to any possible treatment of psychosis", Lacan once again opens the chapter on the Oedipus complex to which he will consecrate four lessons. It is here that we find the developments on what he calls the three times of the Oedipus complex. Here, Lacan attempts to add diachrony to the synchrony of the metaphor, in other words, time to structure, which was also written in the L and R schemas. We see here that Lacan does not repeat himself; if he adds these [three] times, it is because he is advancing towards the construction of the graph of desire which appears at the end of the seminar, and this graph combines the synchrony of language and the structure of speech in its relation to the Other, which unfolds in time. It was already in play in the witticism, which contributed to the same advancement. With the metaphor, there is no longer any need to resort to the myth or to the theatre. The elegant pathways that it traced replaced them. He thus intended to put some order into the consequences of the Freudian Oedipus for the analysts of the time and to remind them of the structural perspective. Lacan says: "We have now come to the point of asking ourselves about the paternal failing [*carence paternelle*]. There are weak fathers, submissive [*soumis*] fathers, subdued fathers, fathers castrated by their wives, and finally infirm fathers, blind fathers, lame fathers, and what have you." It is indeed possible that we are still in this moment of 1957. The metaphor was Oedipus, put in order, in the order of language, but not rejected. I insisted during our last *Journées* on the fact that the metaphor did not correct the normative side of the Freudian Oedipus. I am coming back to it in order to establish this affirmation even more, and I bring it to mind in order to measure where Lacan started from, not only theoretically, but at the level of his own convictions. I am quoting *Les formations de l'inconscient,* pp. 165–166:

> The Oedipus complex has a normative function, not simply in the moral structure of the subject, nor in his relationships with reality, but regarding the assumption [*assomption*] of his sex.
> The question of genitalisation is double: maturation and assumption by the subject of his own sex, in other words to call things by their name, the reason why the man assumes a virile model [*type viril*] and the woman assumes a certain feminine model [*type féminin*], recognises herself as a woman, identifies with her womanly functions. Virility and femininity are the two terms that translate what is essentially the oedipal function.

In the preceding seminar, *La relation d'objet*, we find something even more radical in its conformism; Lacan says that it is not enough for oedipal normativisation to lead to hetero-sexuality, that it is still necessary to be hetero-sexual. I quote, "following the rules", it is necessary that the subject, boy or girl, "get there in such a way that he situates himself correctly with regard to the father" (Lacan, 1998a,

p. 201) – which means being ready to become a father or a mother. Its function was thus explicitly normative: it conditioned, according to Lacan, a compliant, hetero-sexual sexuality, and the normed relationship to reality. Incidentally Lacan was still speaking about the Oedipus complex and in a style that appears stupefying today. But at the time, these remarks didn't surprise anyone. It was the general *doxa* of the IPA, and it guided the norms of the end of analysis, sexed love, heterosexual genitality and assumed [*assumée*] procreation.

The paternal order

To say it another way, the paternal function appeared as the condition, not only of mental health, that is to say of the normal relationship to reality, but also of the adaptation to sexual and moral norms of the established social link [*lien social*]. And, it seems, suspicion was not yet falling upon these norms. Nearly ten years later in "Position of the unconscious", drafted in March 1964, we see that Lacan had already shifted, because he distributes the relation of the sexes between two sides, that of what is living [*du vivant*], with the drives – I won't develop this – and that of the Other, with a capital O. He unfolds this point, saying, the Other, "the locus in which speech is verified as it encounters the exchange of signifiers, the ideals they prop up, the elementary structures of kinship, the metaphor of the father considered as a principle of separation, and the ever-reopened division in the subject owing to his initial alienation – on this side alone and by the pathways I have just enumerated, order and norms must" – I would like to emphasise the norm here – "be instituted which tell the subject what a man or a woman must do" (Lacan, [1964] 2006, p. 720). Imposing itself, then, was the question of knowing if, coming out of this, namely out of the order that has come from the Other, there could be only disorder. All the same, I would like to emphasise that this phrase indicates clearly that the order which has come from the Other, beginning with this period [in Lacan], was not, for Lacan, reduced only to the ideal norms of the Other. Lacan started to realise – the notion of alienation is enough to indicate this – that for the one who speaks there is some order that does not come from norms, and which commands, however, with impossibilities and necessities, an invisible order, that of the logic of language, which imposes itself on the one who speaks. I evoked this last time. Lacan finished by opting for an ethics where "it is logic that commands." This has nothing to do with conformism.

We can say, incidentally, that the writing of the metaphor was already an attempt at getting away from the social norm. With the metaphor, Lacan attempted to write the subordination of the imaginary to the symbolic, and even more, the determination of the imaginary by the symbolic, the very one that he recuses later when he says repeatedly at the time of the Borromean knot that the three consistencies [*consistances*] are autonomous. This point is essential for clinical practice. When we attempt to talk about a case, specifically in the case of a child, do we still postulate this subordination or not? Here the entire chapter on the practical usage of the analytic concepts, at least of those that the clinician has at his disposal, would open up.

The ordering metaphor of the father, I suppose you know how it is written, made it possible – I am using the past tense – made it possible to symbolise the lack of the mother's desire, itself undetermined, by means of the signifier of the phallus. Freud noticed the singular role of the male organ alone in the saids [*dits*] of subjects, those of girls as well as those of boys – thus, in spite of anatomy. Lacan explains this by positing that it is only possible if the organ has passed through the signifier. The father is a metaphor, that is, a signifier substituted for another, because the metaphor is written:

$$\frac{NdP}{DM} \cdot \frac{DM}{x} \bullet NdP \bullet \frac{A}{\varphi}$$

The Other becomes the locus where the phallus is signified. We have translated by saying that the metaphor shifts the mother's lack – the lack symbolised by her absence, meaning the lack which remains for her while she has this object that is the child – from an undetermined lack, to a sexed lack, symbolised by the phallus, which establishes a possible sexual desire for the bearer of the said [*porteur du dit*]. The metaphor of the father was the generator of the phallic signification of desire.

Let me make a remark here to which I will come back later: this does not imply that the metaphor produces the phallic signifier. The thesis is that it makes it appear in the imaginary, Lacan says – when Lacan says signification, it's the Imaginary. It is the general function of the metaphor: it shifts a signifier to the level of the signified. This is how Lacan retranslates Freudian repression, a signifier that has disappeared from the chain of signifiers has become dissimulated, latent Freud would say, in the signified. Hence the paradox of the peerless [*sans pair*] signifier as Lacan called it. What purpose does this phallic signifier serve? According to Lacan, it permits to the little child to match here his living being [*être de vivant*] with his "stupid and ineffable existence". This is what Lacan wrote in his commentary on the R schema: to the Name-of-the-Father in the symbolic, responds the phallic signification in the imaginary.

In my exposé at the last *Journées* of the School, I highlighted how much the Freudian father was syntonic with the structure of the classical family, which is constructed as the social link of the master's discourse (the master's discourse where a semblant, an S_1, that of the head of the family, the father, orders around his other, his wife). It would thus ensure the superposition of two couples, that of the parental social link and the sexed one of man and woman, at the price of a relationship of domination, of legalised domination of the wife [*épouse*] who for every social activity was submissive to marital authorisation, let us not forget this. I indicated that the metaphor was not really at odds with this construction. I'll come back to this in order to support my affirmation because this appears to me to be of the greatest importance at the moment, for both analytic discourse and common discourse.

One could object to my saying this if one keeps with the metaphor itself because Lacan dissociates here the father and the Name-of-the-Father very explicitly, saying that the Name-of-the-Father is not the person but a signifier, and that the presence of a father is in no way necessary for the Signifier to be here; and even, in solidarity with these theses: the symbolic father "is the dead father" according to Freud. It's difficult with this to speak of a relation of familial domination. And it would also have to temper the appeals to the father, to the papa, in the clinic.

However, at the same time, Lacan affirms, in purely signifying terms it is true, that the Name-of-the-Father is the signifier that in the Other, the locus, inscribes the law, the law of the Other. This is an Other of the Other, he says it explicitly in *Les formations de l'inconscient*. In the *Écrits*, he concludes at the end of "On a question prior to any possible treatment of psychosis": "The Name-of-the-Father redoubles in the Other's place the very signifier of the symbolic ternary, insofar as it constitutes the law of the signifier" (Lacan, [1957–1958] 2006, p. 481). In *Les formations de l'inconscient*, he says: "the father is, in the Other, the signifier that represents the existence of the locus of the signifying chain as law" (Lacan, 1998b, p. 196). With that, he does not do away with the relationship of the people father/mother that I called a relationship of domination, he transposes it to the level of signifying structure, which legitimises it in fact since the father of the oedipal trio becomes the bearer of the law. Of course, Lacan recused it very quickly, this father, Other of the Other, and very quickly he asserted: there is no Other of the Other, $S(\cancel{A})$, and this time for reasons of pure logic.

But there's more: the description of the three times of the Oedipus complex in *Les formations de l'inconscient*. They are described as the avatars of the relation of the child first to his mother, then to his father, a relation which passes through speech, of course, and here we confirm unequivocally that the Freudian order of the Oedipus complex is conserved and not subverted. Let me remind you: in the first time, the relation is entirely centred on the mother, on the desire of her desire, and the lure of the identification with the phallus; in the second time the father, certainly invested with the signifier, but also the father who is there, intervenes as prohibitor, no more, no less. This is the father of the law of castration: he deprives the child of the mother, and deprives her of the child: "You will not reintegrate your product"; in the third time, which conditions the right exit [*la bonne sortie*] out of the Oedipus complex, Lacan says, the father makes himself preferential for the mother because he can give – and Lacan specifies that to give is to give what one has, here the phallus. For the boy, this creates a promise – he doesn't have it, but he will have it; for the girl, she doesn't have it, but she will receive it. Here too, these are some developments that Lacan went back on. Namely in disconnecting the oedipal father from the real of castration. This is understandable starting with "The subversion of the subject and the dialectic of desire", and this opens up the immense question of the possible dissociation, or not, of the phallic register and the father, a question that culminates and concludes in "L'étourdit".

All of this then in order to say that the paternal metaphor, with the introduction of the signifier of the Name-of-the-Father, indeed, far from putting into question the oedipal father, founded it, and on the structure of language. It was a first attempt to rationalise the myth, and of course it was of great importance because even if this conceptualisation is insufficient, it emphasised the impact of the symbolic, which Lacan took years to bring out. Recusing the metaphor does not mean recusing the primacy of language. If afterwards, Lacan undoes his metaphor, it is in order to have progressed on this same path of rationalisation, and in passing from the tropes of language, metaphor, and metonymy, to the logic of the order of language, the one that in fact leads him to substitute S(A) for the Other of the Other.

The name of the Thing

The seminar that was planned for the year 1963–1964 was announced as "The Names-of-the-Father". The plural form came as a surprise. I am going to come back to his but I just want to emphasise first that this title which put forward that there are names of the name pointed out an imprecision that was latent at the time of the paternal metaphor where the father was thought of as a metaphor, Lacan says this explicitly. He was thus thought of as a signifier, a signifier which is substituted for another, that of the desire of the mother. And incidentally, Lacan made abundant use of the expression: signifier of the Name-of-the-Father. A name, then, in the function of signifier. Implicitly, the question of the difference and the relationship between the name and the signifier came to be posed.

Between the two signifiers of the metaphor, the disparity is patent because the desire of the mother (DM), is a signifier but not a name. What is more, the effect of the metaphor substitutes for it the signifier of the Other, the locus of the Other. This is what I wrote earlier. It is interesting this signifier desire of the mother, DM. We take it too easily as a given. In fact, Lacan provides us here with an example of the apparition, of the creation of a signifier. We are used to saying, with Lacan, the signifier is in the Other, already there. And well, no, not this one. It only emerges if, starting with a linguistic cell [*cellule langagière*] of signifiers that are indeed in the locus of the Other just like the father or mother, a cell that is minimally illustrated by the couple of the phonemes *Fort/Da*, it only emerges then if this signifying cell produces an effect of symbolisation of the absence of the mother. Mother, when it comes down to it, is the name of the first real, DM is the name of the first hole, produced by the emptying operation of the signifier. When it is produced, the lack makes its entry in the form of the lack that remains in the mother despite the presence of her child, and so the real of the mother is barred, and we can write DM. But in order for this to be the case, it is still necessary that the child give a meaning of absence to this *Fort/Da*, failing which the *Fort/Da* changes nothing. We see it with the autistic child who repeats all sorts of games of alternation, which do not produce the effect of a hole in the real – the symbolised absence is a hole in the real. Lacan has the same thesis for schizophrenia, saying that for the schizophrenic "all of the symbolic is real", which signifies that he does not produce this emptying operation. There are thus two definitions of the Other and two uses of the term symbolic in Lacan's work. The Other as first locus of language, he calls the primordial Other, where the child is welcomed before any operation of language, to be written with a big O. This is already the symbolic in a sense, but when we speak of access to the symbolic, it is not of this Other that we speak because to this Other, there is no access. It precedes you, and it is not lacking for anyone who speaks. Here, we are at the chapter of the emergence of the signifier.

Notes

1 [A *historiole* is a word Lacan has derived from Spinoza that makes of the French word for "story" *(histoire)* something like "the cute little story".]

2 $\dfrac{a}{S_2} \rightarrow \dfrac{\cancel{S}}{S_1}$

3 $\dfrac{S_1}{\cancel{S}} \rightarrow \dfrac{S_2}{a}$

4 [*La grand route de la métaphore*]

Chapter VII

5th March 2014

Diagnoses according to the metaphor

I had stopped at the emergence of the signifier DM (desire of the mother) from the paternal metaphor. We are here at the little explored chapter of the production of signifiers. In the seminar *The Ethics of Psychoanalysis* Lacan had given a definition of the Thing, *das Ding*: it is "the real inasmuch as it suffers from the signifier [*pâtit du signifiant*]". This was his classic thesis on the operating signifier, which can be found right up until his hypothesis in the seminar *Encore*. But he had produced another formula playing on the word: "It's the real inasmuch as it builds the signifier [*bâtit du signifiant*]." I commented on this in 1975 in Lacan's presence. You will not find it in the Seuil edition, it was not included. Perhaps because at the time, the person who transcribed the seminar himself emphasised the antecedence of the symbolic. But this was all the same a very bad reason, because the expression already indicated another side of Lacan's thought, one that culminates around 1975 at the moment of the Borromean knot, at a moment where he talks of the hole of the symbolic. To a question he was asked regarding the place that he would give to the Thing, *das Ding*, in the Borromean knot, he responded that it is the hole of the symbolic. And about this hole he says: a hole coughs things up, and what does it cough up? Names of the father. This is not the same thing as building the signifier. I will come back to this, but the common point is that the Thing, this hole in the real, far from being inert, is productive in the field of language. In our commentaries on Lacan, we are used to the idea that the signifier is already there, in the Other, the place where the signifiers are "to be gotten". Yes, but this does not say that the Other is the cause of signifiers – it is their storehouse [*lieu de dépôt*]. The Other is the place where "speech is deposited" he says in *Encore*, and Lacan specifies: watch out for resonances. Indeed, from the storehouse [*dépôt*] to the dump [*dépotoir*], it's not very far. Letter, litter. Signifiers come from the Thing that speaks, and very early on he wrote: the approach of the unsayable produces the word [*l'approche de l'indicible fait mot*]. In *Encore*, he speaks of the real moving towards the symbolic with the image of the spider weaving its web. Incidentally this is why languages are in constant evolution. And so, I insist, to whom can we impute the emergence of this first signifier DM, a name of the Thing in some respects? We cannot impute it to the Other, the locus, even if in the locus, the speech of the parental others – without which there would not be any locus of the Other – is deposited. Is it necessary to convoke "the unsoundable decision of being" (Lacan, [1946] 2006, p. 145)?[1] Most likely, because without it we would only be marionettes of the Other, who would be the sufficient cause of our symptoms of psychosis, neurosis, or perversion.

In any case, the metaphor already ordered a distribution of clinical structures.

The clinical structures have been described, and described very well, by classical psychiatry, the very psychiatry that the current training of psychiatrists makes us forget. It was a descriptive clinic, which at this level retains its validity, and we have every reason to bring it to mind because the DSMs have replaced it with another clinic, equally descriptive, but this time it is a statistical one. This is worse. Our postulate with Lacan is that the structure of language determines these clinical structures (psychosis, neurosis, and perversion), and thus it is the relationship of the subject with the Other, big O, which accounts for the phenomenological traits that psychiatry described, as I have just shown. Indeed, the metaphor made it possible to distinguish, first of all, cases where this signifier DM is not there, that is to say, where there is no symbolisation of the absence of the mother, which remains in some respects totally real – this ranges from autism to the "said schizophrenic".[2] And then there are cases where DM is there but without the signifier of the father, and the subject is confronted with the *x*, the abyss [*gouffre*] of the opacity of his desire, and this is paranoia, which Lacan regards as being identical to psychosis [*identifie à la psychose*]; and then the cases where, owing to the metaphor, this desire finds its symbol in the phallus with neurosis and perversion.

Subsequently, one of our questions with the end of Lacan's teaching is to know how to transpose this approach, or how to rethink it in terms of the Borromean knot. It's in the fact that structure, let's not forget this: is "that which is not learned from experience". An anti-empiricist thesis, if there ever was one, it does not arise from experience like a fish from the river. Structure is constructed, and one evaluates the validity of the construction by the phenomena that it makes it possible to shed light on and possibly to modify. So, after the structure of language, Lacan constructed the structure of the discourses and he himself gave a new definition of psychosis as "outside discourse", and this is something other than placing it in the function of the metaphor or of the graph of desire. With the Borromean knot, the problem arises again. I'll not develop it, but it appears to me as essential that, at each step, it is necessary to rework or adjust our conception of clinical structures. Otherwise, we are stuck with the clinical catechism of old psychiatry.

The names of the name

Let me come back to the Name-of-the-Father which in the metaphor is substituted for the name of the primordial Thing. In 1963, Lacan had planned on giving the seminar on the Names-of-the-Father, plural, just after the year on *Anxiety*. If they are in the plural, it is necessary to distinguish them from the function, which is unique. A question is circulating in the media, "of what is X the name", ever since Alain Badiou formulated "of what is Sarkozy the name?" It's not a question that one would ask regarding the signifier that represents a subject for another signifier, as a match does for its box, according to the example that Lacan uses in *The Ethics of Psychoanalysis*, if my memory is correct. At most we will say that it is the sign of a subject. Lacan really developed this in "Radiophonie", *Encore*, and *Television*. When we say of a word, and not necessarily a proper name, "of what is it the name?", we are not questioning its meaning, its signified, *Sinn*, Frege says. We aim directly at a referent, the referent that we know the signifier misses, the signifier that only produces some signified, *lecton (λεκτὸν)*, the Stoics used to say.

So then, the names? What is the difference between the name and the signifier? And why in his metaphor did Lacan say "Name-of-the-Father" there where he describes a signifier function, which obliges him to say "signifier of the Name-of-the-Father"? For the signifier, we have a precise thesis: it has a signified-effect [*effet de signifié*], whether in metaphor or in metonymy. To these two elements, signifier, signified, it is necessary to add the referent, namely the signifiable, as Lacan was saying at one point. This tripartition comes from the Stoics who Lacan evokes on several occasions, and it can be found in Saussure but also in Frege. The Stoics were bothered by the signified, λεκτὸν, because their doctrine posited that everything is body. If we say the following phrase, "Dion is walking", this is the classic example, the level that we call signifying is perceptible. Even if one doesn't speak French, one hears the sounds or sees the writing. This is of the body. Dion as referent, the thing which is walking, is also a perceptible body. But the meaning of the phrase, the λεκτὸν, is not heard by the ears, not seen by the eyes, not perceived by the senses, hence the Stoic thesis that the meaning of a phrase or of a word, is something incorporeal, and which creates a problem for them. Frege took up the distinction between meaning, *Sinn*, and referent. We also say denotation – Lacan employs the term – in its difference with connotation which is of the order of the signifier. The referent is what is aimed at in discourse. What is aimed at in discourse is of the real. Lacan relied heavily upon Frege's elaborations starting with his text "The signification of the phallus", subtitled "Die Bedeutung des Phallus", and he goes back to it year after year right up to the writing of the phallic function, the basis of the formulas of sexuation in "L'étourdit". The signifier and the name are distinguished with respect to the referent. The signifier produces the signified but owing to this very fact, it misses the referent. Covering it over, enveloping it with the signified, it represses it. In this way, we grasp its difference with the name. The name pins the referent and has no meaning. We can even say that a signifier has no referent. This is what we mean when we say that it is equivocal, namely that it always points back to another signifier, and thus to another signification. A name, on the other hand, has no meaning. It means nothing. It indexes. It pins. This is a given for what we call the proper name. It designates one and only one referent, regardless of what it is. The proper name is an index. But this is more general. The name does predicate: when you say *horse*, that doesn't say anything about what a horse is unless you convoke other signifiers that attribute qualities to it. Between the name and the named, there is no relationship. The arbitrariness that Saussure attributed to the signifier, it is rather to the name that it must be applied. This is why we can ask "of what is this name the name?"

In saying the Names-of-the-Father, plural, Lacan indicates – he specified it – that he already had an idea of possible *suppléances* for the Name-of-the-Father. Of what are these names the name? These are the names of a function that was already addressed by the name father [*nom de père*], and right up until the end, the whole issue is going to be to define this function. We have various terms. We talk of the function of separation from the primordial object in order to designate its operation in what Freud described as the Oedipus Complex, and that Lacan attempted to describe anew in his three times of the Oedipus Complex. Then a function of "saying [*dire*]" starting with "L'étourdit", and finally a function of naming, of [the] saying of naming [*de dire de nomination*]. I am going to follow this development, but already we see that if the function has several names, it means that it can be carried by others besides fathers such as they are defined in what is our discourse, where the father is implicated in sex and generation. But in this case, why still call the function paternal? This is a question that I am going to leave in suspense but to which I will return.

Function of the exception

In any case, it is a function of the exception. In common language, the most general formula for designating an exception is: all but one. It is thus that Freud, without knowing it, constructed his father of the horde in *Totem and Taboo*: all are deprived, all the males are deprived of sexual jouissance, except the primal father, the *pérorant outang* [perorating utang] as Lacan says in "L'étourdit". Lacan pointed out some differences between the said Oedipus complex and *Totem and Taboo*, but there is nevertheless a homology. With regard to the father of the cute little story [*historiole*] of the oedipal trio, we can say the same of the kids, in any case the sons, all of them being deprived of the jouissance of the mother, except the father. There is yet another homology, two moments are distinguished: first of all, a privation of jouissance, then a possibility of jouissance. In the one case, beyond the murder of the father, the sons will have jouissance within the limits of the Law, that is to say, not the unlimited jouissance (enjoyment) of all the women, which incidentally is impossible, but of a few of them. In the other case, with the three times of the Oedipus complex that Lacan brought out so clearly in *Les formations de l'inconscient*: privation in the present, but, as I said, the promise of jouissance in the future, still within the limits of the law. I insist on this in order to stress that the idea of the father-exception is Freudian, even if it is actually Lacan who, following him, after the metaphor, turned to logic in order to explore more rationally what an exception is.

In the metaphor, however, the Name-of-the-Father is already situated as a signifier of exception, although Lacan does not use the term at this time. But after having written his metaphor whose result produces the barred A, to be written:

$$\frac{A}{\varphi}$$

I have reminded you that he is looking to specify the function of this signifier of the Father. He said that it is at the place [*place*] of the Other, hear in this "the locus of signifiers", which he inscribed in his L and R schemas, and he adds in the post-script: "To move on now to the principle of foreclosure [*Verwerfung*] of the Name-of-the-Father, it must be admitted that the Name-of-the-Father redoubles in the Other's place the very signifier of the symbolic ternary, insofar as it constitutes the law of the signifier" (Lacan, [1957–1958] 2006, p. 481).

Let me comment on this. The Other being the locus of all the signifiers, this phrase says clearly that the father is, in the Other, a signifier of exception compared to all of the other signifiers – an exception constitutive of the law of the signifier, and thus an Other of the Other, I said. This latter affirmation, which says that the law is the law of the signifier, already appears to me to be fat with future developments, for as little as Lacan progresses in what he calls here the law of the signifier. But at the moment when he writes this text, the law of the signifier is the law of the production of the signified by the signifier, specifically of the production of signification, provided there is a "button tie" of the chain. This makes of the Name-of-the-Father the button tie of language, which makes it possible to produce signification, the great phallic signification. It's what he writes in the R schema, on page 462 of the *Écrits*. I would also like emphasise the "it must be admitted", in other words it was a hypothesis, a construction, if you like. It is on this point that Lacan is going to change very quickly, not on the signifier of the Name-of-the-Father, but on its place. The change is explicit starting with "The subversion of the subject and the dialectic of desire". It is here that he corrects what he thought he had to admit, the father as Other of the Other, and from here on out he hammers home that there is no Other of the Other, and that "the oedipal show cannot run indefinitely" (Lacan, [1960b] 2006, p. 688). I am insisting on something that is perhaps well-known to many, but I think it is essential to not be content with enumerating the successive theses of Lacan, but rather to grasp what founds this succession, failing which, periodisation gives the impression of something arbitrary.

If he recuses the Other of the Other, it is in the name of what the logic of sets teaches us, and Lacan often refers himself to the paradoxes raised by Bertrand Russel on this subject, and specifically to that of the catalogue of catalogues, and above all to Gödel's theorem on the incompleteness of every consistent system. What he learned from it is that one cannot constitute a multiplicity of elements in a set – in other words, to make an all [*tout*] of them – which would make it possible to say all, whatever they may be, all of the signifiers, all men, etc., without an element being outside of the set. This usage will be explicit in "L'étourdit", but it is already present, I think, in "The subversion of the subject and the dialectic of desire", with the writing of S(A̸), which can be situated as a (−1) with respect to the set of all signifiers. I'll not comment on this complex passage which mixes implicit logical references with more explicit linguistic references, and which attempts to articulate language with jouissance and with construction. This is not my intention here. What I am highlighting is that starting from this point, he writes the Other, the locus, as a holed locus [*lieu troué*], and not saturated by the Name-of-the-Father, which will have consequences in the thesis of the oedipal father symptom, and above all, starting with this text, he dissociates the father from castration. I insisted on the fact that the seminar *Anxiety* develops this theme of a castration that does not come from the father but from the grasp [*prise*] of language, but this dissociation is already present in "The subversion of the subject and the dialectic of desire", where the father is presented as a solution: he unites a desire with the law. We are still however on the subject of the effect of the father on the normed regulation of jouissances, with which Lacan began in a very traditional, even conformist way. I have insisted quite a lot on this point.

The saying as exception

It is in "L'étourdit" that the function of the paternal exception is most highlighted and the logical references most explained. In fact, the references to logic are multiple: at once to the classical logic of Aristotle in order to mark the limits of it, to the logic of Frege, and to the logic of sets. They would merit a separate study, which I am not going to do, because I am pursuing my question. In this text, the function of the father is reduced to a function of a logical exception. We often say this. However, this exception is rethought here, not as a signifier but as a saying [*dire*]. It is thus no longer a signifying function, but a discursive one. There is no discourse that does not make use of the language apparatus or include it in its structure − obviously − but discourse is another structure that not only adds the jouissance element to the signifiers but which also, apart from these terms S_1, S_2, $, a$, supposes places, and notably the place of the semblant. And this place supposes the saying [*dire*].

In "L'étourdit", there are two developments on the saying as exception: one that concerns the saying in general and one that concerns the father in particular, who is also an exception, but not just any exception. I'll start with the first one.

"That one says remains forgotten … [*Qu'on dise reste oublié*]", Lacan says. This phrase has more philosophical bearing that one imagines. It is a fatal phrase for any metaphysics, because to whoever says "being is", it responds: you said it. The consequence for psychoanalysis: Lacan proposes as a minimum of interpretation the "I am not making you say it [*je ne te le fais pas dire*]", which targets not what was said, but one's saying [*dire*]. The saying as an act of the use of language does arise from the signifier. It is, I often repeat, ex-sistential. "A moment of ex-sistence" situated from discourse [*situé du discours*], Lacan says. This saying is the enunciation as act of enunciation, the fact of pronouncing or not. One decides to speak or not. Let me specify that the enunciation as act of saying is not to be confused with the unconscious enunciation as repressed signifying chain – repressed *via* metaphor and metonymy – and which is deciphered in the chain of speech. This enunciation as chain, which Lacan writes in the upper level of his graph is the reason why I always say more than I think I am saying, but it is yet necessary that I say [*que je dise*].

Of the saying [*dire*] in general, let us put forth that it ex-sists to the saids [*dits*]. It is not included among them. It is not an element among the saids, not an additional said. It is the condition of saids articulated in language, in other words, of statements [*énoncés*]. The said does not go without saying, and what remains forgotten, says Lacan, is that one says. Forgotten "in what is said of what is heard [*dans ce qui se dit de ce qui s'entend*]". How can we hear this "what is heard"? We can take it as what is heard with the ears, namely the hearing of signifiers in the auditory sense, but also what is heard (or understood) with comprehension.[3] Remember, Lacan said: what I have to grasp "is about comprehension". In this case, what is heard is what I am going to decipher from the unconscious repressed chain, but, in both cases, what is heard are the saids articulated as signifiers. These articulated saids which are heard, which have the structure of language, do not go without saying, which implies that they place themselves in a discourse, in the structure of a discourse. So, what is said, at the place of the signified, in these saids? Truth, Lacan says, namely "the Freudian Thing such as I situated it as being the said of truth". The saids pose as truth, by definition, they suppose a subject, whatever they may say, but "for a said to be true, it is yet necessary that one say it, that there be a saying". "The saying is not the dimension of truth", "it escapes the said". The subject "is an effect of a said", whereas the "signified" of the saying "is only ex-sistence to the said".

However, from this saying, as moment of ex-sistence, Lacan moves on to the saying as "One-saying [*Un-dire*]"; no longer the verb, but the substantive: the saying of Freud, the saying of the analysand to be made to ex-sist, the saying that makes man, the saying of the not-all [*pas-toute*]. Regarding this saying, the substantive one, we can raise two questions: how can we define it precisely once it cannot be formulated in a statement? And how do we access it? Lacan responds to both questions, although he does not formulate it in this way. The saying is demonstrated as a "*dire que non* [saying that no]". The expression has created a lot of misunderstanding. However, he was very specific about what the *dire que non* is: "It is containing [*le contien*] that one grasps here, not contradiction, – response, not the resumption of negation, – rejection, not correction. To respond in this way suspends what the said has of something true" (Lacan, 1973, p. 9), but in excepting itself, this One-saying constitutes as a set all of the saids to which it ex-sists. Lacan speaks incidentally in "… ou pire" of the One-saying which is manifested as ex-sisting. Application: it concerns interpretation. First of all, the interpretation by means of equivocation that he developed in "L'étourdit". It is an interpretation that in any case suspends the dimension of truth in diffracting it, if I may so. And the little text "… ou pire", which I have just mentioned, poses that interpretation responds to the One-saying of demand, this real of "the One all alone [*Un tout seul*]" of the analysand.

My second question was: how can we approach this saying? By inference, when it comes to the saying of Freud. "The saying of Freud is inferred from logic which takes at its source the said of the unconscious. It is inasmuch as Freud discovered this said that it ex-sists." The said of the unconscious, the half-said [*mi-dit*] of the unconscious, nowhere announces any sexual relationship – of the sexual relationship "there is only a statement". In *Encore*, Lacan will pass from what cannot be said to what cannot be written, but that is not the problem here. This saying of Freud is consubstantial with analytic discourse.

From the structure of language to that of discourse, there are many changes, namely the taking into account of the saying, an ex-sistential one, which I have just mentioned. But meaning also changes meaning. Have we noticed this? It is important when one defines the real as "outside meaning [*hors sens*]". In language, meaning is a kind of signified, a surplus of signified next to this other signified that is signification, which is produced by a chain, S_1/S_2. He says that to me, but "What does he want?" Meaning is thus the meaning of desire. The graph of "The subversion of the subject and the dialectic of desire" inscribes it as signified of the unconscious chain. Freud's practice of interpretation can be entirely situated in this register. It aims at the truth of desire, which is incidentally linked to the drives, but that does not change this point. When it is a question of discourses, Lacan's little quadripods, I quote: "Meaning is only produced from the translation of one discourse into another." In other words, it depends on the term that comes to the place of the semblant. Antinomy of meaning and signification, the meaning is not a signified of language. It depends on the term that is in the place of the semblant in discourse. Each discourse is thus interpreted by another or from another, which in putting another term at the place of the semblant, makes appear what was aimed at in discourse and what in this discourse we didn't know. These phrases, which seem bothersome when Lacan says in *Encore*, "at each change of discourse, a new love", at each change of discourse, there is a something of an analytic discourse, are clarified from this. Yes, because the change of discourse produces an effect of interpretation, the new semblant giving meaning to the old one.

Notes

1 [The French *insondable* could perhaps also be translated as "unfathomable"].
2 [In "L'étourdit", Lacan makes reference to "*le dit schizophrène*", which can also be translated either as "the schizophrenic to whom I am referring" or "the supposed schizophrenic" (Lacan, 1973, p. 31).]
3 [In French *entendre* means both "to hear" and "to understand", and *entendement*, the noun form, means "understanding": *Comment entendre ce qui s'entend? On peut le prendre comme ce qui s'entend avec les oreilles, soit l'écoute des signifiants au sens auditif, mais aussi bien ce qui s'entend avec l'entendement.*]

Chapter VIII

19th March 2014

I stopped last time on the fact that the construction of the structure of the discourses brought a new perspective on the question of meaning, but I didn't have time to develop it. In the part of "L'étourdit" that starts with this phrase "let us put into motion the matter of meaning",[1] you will notice that what Lacan says about it is not what has been said since the Stoics, which Lacan used a great deal, namely that meaning is one of the signifieds of a chain of language, the other being signification, and this is what is written in the graph of desire. But a discourse is not only a structure of language. It supposes places where elements of language lodge themselves, notably the place that Lacan calls the place of the semblant. The nature of the discourse is decided according to the term that lodges itself in this place. S_1 for the master's discours, $\$$ for the hysteric's discourse, etc. What decides the term is the saying [*dire*] as an act that is at once implicit and constituent, and which is not of the order of language. The meaning of a discourse only appears on the basis of another discourse, namely of another saying [*dire*] (Lacan, 1973, pp. 36–37). "Antinomy of meaning and signification." Signification is determined by grammar, is inherent to a chain of language. The meaning of a discourse escapes this discourse. Lacan takes the example of Kant: when the meaning of Kant's saids [*dits*] is raised, they have no more signification. "They only maintained the signification as long as they didn't have meaning, not even the common meaning." He already demonstrated it in *Kant with Sade*. Kant's *Critique of Pure Reason* with its promotion of the grand signification of the universality of the moral law, which is only universal because it eliminates all pathological motives, takes its meaning from Sade's discourse, from a Sadean fantasy.

The final pages of "Radiophonie" (Lacan, 1970, pp. 96–98) already highlighted how a discourse is clarified, which is to say, how it takes its meaning from another discourse. The master's discourse is clarified from the hysteric's discourse. When the patient moves to the place of the agent – when the S_1, which was at the place of the other in the hysteric's discourse moves to the place of the agent – it is because "he gives up on responding as a man" to the hysterical beckoning [*sollicitation*]. The master's discourse maintains itself in [*s'entretient*], and thus stems from the hysteric's discourse. In the same way, the university discourse is clarified from analytic discourse – when the patient, written "*a*" in the place of the little other in the university discourse, moves to the place of the agent, knowledge moves to the place of truth, and thus the obscurantism inherent to the university discourse, its indifference to truth, appears. Each discourse interprets another discourse, gives it meaning – what is looked for in the one clarifying what the other avoids. It is always castration that is avoided, the castration that is played out between the hysteric's discourse and the master's discourse at the level of sex, or the castration that is played out between university discourse and analytic discourse at the level of the relation to truth, because there is only one relationship with truth: castration (Lacan, 1970, p. 94).

The new formulation is not contradictory to the meaning of desire in speech since discourse orders speech – one always speaks in an established discourse. When Lacan says discourse without speech, this signifies that it is not speech alone that decides the term that orders the link. On the contrary, we "*s'apparole*" to a discourse.[2] Moreover, it is obvious at the beginning of each analysis, the subject comes in order to "*s'apparoler*" to what is for him a new discourse. In fact, this is what the notion of "subjective rectification" actually means. The meaning of speech depends on the discourse from which one pronounces it.

No discourse of *suppléance*

Let me take up the thread of my question about what we can conclude from "L'étourdit" concerning the Oedipus complex and the father. The conception of discourses, which are organised social links, Lacan produced it in *The Other Side of Psychoanalysis*, wrote it in "Radiophonie", and completed it in "L'étourdit". I mention this in order to stress the point that this has nothing to do as such with the question of the father and the Oedipus Complex. But the function of the saying *(dire)* developed in "L'étourdit" helps him to reformulate the function of the Freudian father. Notice the problem that he must resolve at this moment. It is very precise. Once there is no programmed sexual relationship, programmed neither by the singular unconsciouses nor by a discourse, there is no discourse that would not be of a semblant. How can we nevertheless obtain the two heterosexual halves?

One could hope that a discourse stands in [*supplée*] for the non-relationship. The title of the preceding seminar *D'un discours qui ne serait pas du semblant* was meant to say that there was no such discourse that could explain beyond the ideals of sex – that is to say the signifiers of sex – that could explain, then, the links of two sexed bodies. They are outside discourse. We are not speaking here of subjects, but of bodies that enjoy [*corps jouissants*] as consubstantial with so-called sexuality.

It is necessary to obtain "the identifications with the man half and the woman half", as he says on page 14 – at least, as I have pointed out, it is necessary in order for there to be reproductive sexuality. This is explicit in the text. For this, Freud convoked the story of Oedipus and the identifications that it makes possible. As for Lacan, he announces to us that he is going to produce, I quote: "The logic from which are articulated castration and the Oedipus complex in analysis." Let me highlight here, "in analysis" – he does not say "in civilisation". I'll leave this point in abeyance. If we talk of "articulating castration and the Oedipus complex", this supposes that these are two autonomous realties because if the first were the consequence of the second, if castration were the effect of the Oedipus complex, this would not be an articulation. And in fact, starting with "The subversion of the subject and the dialectic of desire", and thus before *Anxiety*, Lacan already separated the Oedipus complex and castration – on one side a myth, on the other an effect of language. This logic which articulates castration and the Oedipus Complex is given by the first two formulas of sexuation (Lacan, 1973, p. 14); after introducing them, Lacan concludes a few paragraphs later: "The Oedipus complex is what I say, not what one thinks" (Lacan, 1973, p. 16).

The reformulated Oedipus complex is limited to the first two formulas, then, if it is what he says it is, and so, it is not for all who speak but only for the man half at best. The Oedipus complex did not make it possible to obtain two halves but only one. As early as 1993, in the *Journées* dedicated to "The beyond of the Oedipus complex", I pointed out that the first occurrence of this beyond is the side that is called woman. Lacan even diagnoses a "slipping [*glissement*]" of Freud who was wrong to implicate women, to apply the same measuring rod to them as to the "for-all men [*pourtout homme*]", and he adds: this is the "scandal of analytic discourse". An inevitable question arises: does this logification of the hetero-sexual norm of the Oedipus complex shift – and to say norm is to say that it comes from the symbolic – does this then shift the norm from the symbolic to the real? If yes, logifying would amount, not to relativising or tempering the oedipal norm, but to founding it as ineliminable, because the real cannot be transgressed. More generally, the question is one of knowing whether the phallic function is subordinated to the father, like the metaphor indicated for phallic signification, with consequences for psychosis. I am going to treat this point in detail.

Thus, depending on the reading that one does of "L'étourdit", one will conclude either on a strong necessity of the father as the regulator of sex and the relationship to reality – and in which case, without the father, there is no hope for our societies – or one will conclude the opposite, that we can do without the father. The clinical stakes are huge and the Lacanian movement is divided on this point.

Let me first make a few contextual remarks about what comes before "L'étourdit", and about what follows because this seems to me to already indicate an orientation for laying out the path from the starting to the end-point.

Before, after

The text is from July 1972. It is just after "… ou pire", and just before *Encore*. What theses do we have at our disposal prior to this? Prior to this, Lacan formulated his "there is no such thing as a sexual relationship". There are two sexes but only one function, the phallic function, which, all by itself, objects to the relationship. It is, however, implicated in the relations between the sexes by means of the identifications that it makes possible with having or with being the phallus, but in everything that precedes "L'étourdit", this function only presides over the typology of the appearing as man or woman, although phallic lack also presides over sexual desire (c.f. the three-card monte man). This says nothing, however, about "sexual" jouissance, that of coitus, jouissance written with a capital Phi, which remains "impossible to negativise" according to the formula of "The subversion of the subject."

The formula from "Radiophonie", "there is no such thing as a sexual relationship", does not concern the comedy of the sexes but the real of their jouissances at the moment of truth. It designates the failing [*manque*] to state, as much as to write, a relationship of jouissance [*un rapport de jouissance*]. As a result, every regulation of the relations between the sexes as an effect of discourse, every regulation by a semblant, the father of the family and his spouse, the king, the queen, all of these signifiers that are constitutive of social links, miss the dimension of sexed, body-to-body encounters, because for them, for the bodies, there is no semblant that creates a discourse, a social link. This is what Lacan put forward in *D'un discours qui ne serait pas du semblant*: there is no discourse of the real of sexual jouissance. This is perfectly coherent with the fact that has prevailed until now, namely that these body relations have been relegated to private life, as we say, to the secret alcove of cottages, or brothels. Incidentally, it is amusing that, when bodies and their relations are today displayed everywhere, and have come out of secrecy and the unrepresentable, we still want to protect intimacy, whereas the foundation of this very notion of intimacy was relegation – there is no other word for it – of bodies of jouissance. Now we've come to the point of considering as intimacy what is said in the office of the president of the republic, thus confusing political secrets with intimacy proper, which implies the body. The next step led Lacan, in "… ou pire", to formulate "*Y a d'l'Un*". In fact, two writings accompany the seminar "… ou pire", in which is put forward the crucial thesis "*Y a d'l'Un*", which means *de l'Un* (of the One) that objects to the One of Eros, about which we dream and which would be the union of the sexes. These two writings of which I am speaking are the little text at the beginning of *Scilicet 5* entitled "… ou pire" and "L'étourdit." *Y a d'l'Un* – this is consonant with what capitalism, outside psychoanalysis, produces – which capitalism prescribes nothing, neither in matters of love nor in matters of sex – and with the evolution of morals there where capitalism triumphs, an evolution which is undeniable and convergent with what Lacan promotes there. Let me summarise the three preceding steps: no such thing as a sexual relationship, no such thing as a discourse of *suppléance*, *Y a d'l'Un*. It would be surprising with what I am bringing up here that the logified formulas of the Freudian Oedipus complex would be made for bringing back the couple of the Oedipus complex, which I have said was not only sexual but social. "L'étourdit" attempts to account, with a fresh perspective, for the fact that despite this *Y a d'l'Un*, there are hetero-sexual couples – which, after all, in no way arises from necessity. We are starting to notice this.

As for what comes after "L'étourdit", what direction is indicated? The solution to the non-relationship, stated clearly in *R.S.I.* where it is a matter of bringing bodies together, is the symptom. Singular symptoms coming from the unconscious – which for each individual are a solution in presiding over what is established for him concerning bodily relations – I don't know if I should say between the sexes or simply between sexed bodies. This thesis of the symptom-partner [*partenaire symptôme*] is explicit in *R.S.I.*, in the lesson of January 21st 1975, and as a result, the norm of oedipal hetero-sexuality itself appears as a symptom that is not at all logically necessary. With the symptom such as Lacan defines it, we are beyond any collective norm, even if it is a paternal one. Not forgetting all of the explicit formulas regarding the Name-of-the-Father – a name to lose [*nom à perdre*] – regarding the "doing without the father". Thus, I say that with what frames "L'étourdit", with what comes before it and which I have just brought out in broad brush strokes, as much as with what comes after, it would indeed be strange should the logification of the Oedipus complex aim to reinforce it, as I think the metaphor did.

The function (Φx)

Let me go back to the formulas of sexuation. The saying [*dire*] in general is an exception, which ex-sists to the saids [*dits*], which is then a *dire que non* to the saids of truth. From here, Lacan defines the exception of the father as a specific "*dire que non*", because it is a *dire que non* to the function Φx. He aims to give here the logic of the exception that Freud described in *Totem and Taboo*, the question being one of knowing the significance of this logification. It would be surprising if it aimed to endorse the father since he makes fun of the comedy of the perorating utang [*pérorant outang*].

The writing of the function Φx is as such a new addition, resulting from the two preceding seminars, but Lacan explicitly and without interruption connects it to what he had developed, practically since the beginning, concerning the role of the phallus, written at that time in lowercase, in the relation between the sexes.

Phallic signification

The phallic signifier, written in lowercase, was the signifier, I quote, "destined to designate meaning effects [*effets de signifiés*] as a whole, insofar as the signifier conditions them by its presence as signifier" (Lacan, [1958b] 2006, p. 579). The major effect that the signifier has the power to produce is the effect of lack from where desire sustains itself. As a result, this phallic signifier has an identificatory function. It makes it possible to identify the stupid existence of the little subject, thus to knot this existence to the desire of the Other, which, according to Lacan at this time, had an impact on the field of reality. And then, it presides over sexed identifications which make it possible to place oneself, or not, on the side of one's own anatomical sex. Neither the real of the organism, nor the anatomical image makes man and woman. It is a symbolic affair, thus an affair of the subject, for the male and female halves, which participate at once in the real and the imaginary, to become man or woman from the moment that this is articulated in language, and it requires an identification with the man half or the woman half. This thesis from 1958 is taken up with no change in "L'étourdit", on page 14 (Lacan, 1973). The identification with a sex goes through the symbolic, but language has only one signifier concerning sex, namely, the phallus. This is Freud's discovery, which Lacan rethought for a long time. We can see the problem: it is a question, as Freud said in 1915 in a footnote in the *Three Essays on the Theory of Sexuality*, of elucidating the problem of the very possibility of hetero-sexuality. In other words, for Lacan in 1972, how can we make two, the two of a relation of sexed jouissances, with this signifier alone, or with a single function? He responded to this question, and he repeats here, I quote, we can "ascribe to the being or having the phallus (c.f. my *Bedeutung* from *Écrits*) the function that stands in for the sexual relationship". Signification belongs to the register of imaginary effects of the symbolic, of the signifier. This is how the paternal metaphor situated the phallus, as a signifier that gave a sexual signification to the desire of the mother. Lacan named it "signification" – he then placed signification in the Imaginary – as an effect of the signifier of the father. This can be read explicitly in the R schema:

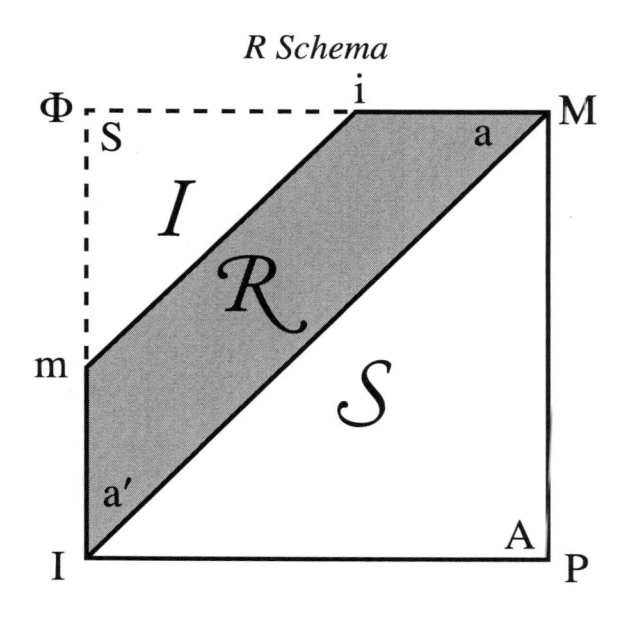

R Schema

This is well known. I developed it in detail in *What Lacan Said about Women*. In calling the function Φ*x*, written with an uppercase Phi, what does Lacan add? Is the phallic signification of 1958, the one that is supposed to be lacking in psychosis, the same thing as the phallic function of 1972? A second question would be to measure the significance of the fact that he writes it as a propositional function in the style of Frege. He first of all said, "signification of the phallus", the *Bedeutung* being in the subtitle. And this is what we say all the time. However, the subtitle *Bedeutung*, appearing in 1958, was not only there because Lacan had read his text in German. It already indicated, I think, that he was not totally satisfied with this term signification because *Bedeutung*, according to Frege, from whom we get this term, is not the signified, it is the referent. I will come back to this.

The jouissance of the phallus

The phallus written with an uppercase Phi, beginning with "The subversion of the subject and the dialectic of desire", writes jouissance. This is not in contradiction with what comes before, it is a complement. It concerns the jouissance at play at the sexual level when "sexual" desire operates and brings bodies together. Indeed, note that what was missing in "The signification of the phallus" was the consideration of properly sexual jouissance. It was just like in fairy tales. We explained how the couple is formed but we said nothing about what followed, what came after ... They get married and have lots of children ... It was a question only of the identification with man or woman through having or being the phallus, which presides over what I often evoke as the comedy of the sexes because this phallic signification projects, as Lacan says, all of "the ideal or typical manifestations of each of the sexes' behaviour" (Lacan, [1958b] 2006, p. 582) in appearing, the feminine masquerade and the masculine parade. This function of the imaginary between male and female beings exists even in the animal world. The entire field of ethology attests to this. All the more reason to cease thinking, as Lacan did with the Borromean knot, that the imaginary is subordinate to the symbolic. However, there is a clause. He says "comedy": "including the act of copulation itself" (Lacan, [1958b] 2006, p. 582).[3] The clause marks the place of the question to come, that of the jouissance linked to this act at the moment of truth.

What characterises this phallic jouissance is that it falls within the scope of castration. Depending on the text, we see Lacan saying "function of jouissance" or "function of castration". It's one and the same thing because it is a jouissance that he sometimes calls "castrated." It bears the trait of the cut, a cut on the surface of the body. It is localised and also temporally cut because it is discontinuous. Over the course of his elaborations, starting in the 1970s, let us say after the *Écrits*, Lacan produced many formulas on this subject, all of which are convergent.

At the sexual level, it is the jouissance that shouldn't be, the one which objects to the relationship, and which at the same time stands in for it [*y supplée*]. The jouissance about which one can say, "that's not it" is a formula of the "wail of the call to the real" (Lacan, 1973, p. 8),[4] Lacan says. The thesis being that castration is not to be identified with the failures of the act – it is inherent to its success. The success of the act makes the failure of the relationship. The seminar on *Anxiety* put a lot of emphasis on this theme. In *Encore*, Lacan connects this sexual castration, which has nothing to do with the threat of scissors, to the fact that this jouissance is displaced in language, speaks of something else [*parle d'autre chose*], as he puts it. The "that's not it" supposes the jouissance of which it would be a question if that were it – in other words, if there were a relationship – but it supposes yet another. Which one? That of speech, and Lacan goes on to evoke the *Three Essays* and the *Trieb* of Freud, the drift [*dérive*] of drive jouissance as a test of the non-relationship (Lacan, 1999, p. 112). The "Where it speaks, it enjoys [*là ou ça parle, ça jouit*]", stems from the gap inscribed in the sexual (Lacan, 1999, p. 115). "The other satisfaction", the satisfaction of speech, from the drift of drive jouissance, Lacan says that it is the satisfaction "that answers to phallic jouissance". Is phallic jouissance itself present in speech, in language? Yes, it is ciphered as a one that repeats. This couple of phallic jouissance and drive jouissance is in play in repetition. This is what I showed the year that I worked on this theme. All of this to say that the "closed field" of the sexual relation is not a ghetto for phallic jouissance. It is a jouissance that circulates in the field of language.

It is a jouissance that we represent to ourselves as power, Lacan says in *Le sinthome*. We could then add "inversely to its real function", which is castration. However, it is a fact that as soon as we talk about the phallic, we think of power, in every domain – politics, art, love, sex, etc. It is the jouissance that supports, in a fundamental way, all of the undertakings that aim at making for oneself ... a stepladder [*escabeau*]. The stepladder is the instrument, I could say, of narcissism, although today I'd rather say an instrument of the competitive One. The competitive One is not the One of singularity; because it is competitive, it is among others that it endeavours to outclass. At one time, we called the stepladder sublimation, but very early on, especially in *The Ethics of Psychoanalysis*, Lacan reduced the idealising overtone that this term has in Freud, and this notion of the stepladder is the culmination of this renovation of the term sublimation.

The question that remains is one of knowing where this phallic jouissance comes from and whether it supposes the father.

Notes

1 [*mettons en train l'affaire du sens*]
2 [Here, the neologism *s'apparoler* refers to another neologism, *l'apparole*, which can be found in: Lacan, J. (2001a [1970]). Préface à une thèse. In: *Autres écrits*. Paris: Éditions du Seuil, p. 398.]
3 [This translation could also read "right up to the limit of the act of copulation itself".]
4 [*vagissement de l'appel au réel*]

Chapter IX

2nd April 2014

I had gotten to the question of knowing where phallic jouissance comes from. The question is one of knowing if it is subordinate to the father as Lacan said of the imaginary signification of the phallus. The answer is no, although we repeat thinking that we are drawing from Lacan, that the phallic function is missing when the function of the father is missing, and specifically in psychosis. This thesis comes from the time of the paternal metaphor and of the R schema. But Lacan spoke then, with the term phallic function that he was already using, about the phallus as signifier of desire's lack. Next, he included in this function the uppercase phallus of jouissance. He introduces it in "The subversion of the subject and the dialectic of desire", the same text where he already dissociates castration and paternal function, as I have said, a theme that he will take up again in *Anxiety*. I am not going to follow all of the ins and outs of this development but I will skip to the end of them where the thesis is explicit in *Le sinthome*. We can see incidentally that in "L'étourdit" the phallic function is introduced before the father function and independently of it – but this is no more than a clue. In *Le sinthome*, Lacan redefines this jouissance, distinguishes it from that of the penis, but above all he explains the origin of it, and it is not the father, it is … speech. The function of speech must then be rewritten.

Speech as cause

"We think we are male because we have a little waggly tail", he says, but "more is needed" (Lacan, 2005, p. 15). What more? For a long time, we have known that the phallus was necessary here, the one that we thought didn't come without the father. But here is Lacan saying explicitly: the phallus, that is, "the conjunction of what I called this *parasite*, which is the little waggly tail in question, with the function of speech" (Lacan, 2005, p. 15). This is moreover how he had, a few months earlier, situated the precocious formation of symptoms as a conjunction, and more than a conjunction, a "coalescence" of the *matérialité* of the unconscious that comes from spoken *lalangue* with sexual reality, that of the little waggly tail, which he specified in illustrating it with the case of little Hans. Taken literally, these developments undo the solidarity between the phallic signifier and the father – unless we say that there is no speech without the father. I will come back to this!

Phallic jouissance is constituted, he says, "at the conjunction of the symbolic with the real [...]". It is distinguished from that of the penis – about which he is also specific – which plays out in eroticism with respect to the imaginary of the body and its orifices. The seminar *Le sinthome* states this very clearly. To say "orifice" obviously convokes the jouissance of the polymorphous drives and is to say that the penis marches to the beat of the drive. On the other hand, concerning the jouissance of the phallus, Lacan says: "It is the place of what is, in consciousness, designated by the speaking-being [*parlêtre*] as power" (Lacan, 2005, p. 56). Power of what? Power of words, which on occasion give sexual power to the penis, the little waggly tail, but this goes much further. Indeed, he adds for "the speaking-being [*parlêtre*], [...] there is the power to conjoin speech and what there is of a certain jouissance, that which is supposedly of the phallus and experienced as parasitic, from the fact of this speech itself [...]".

It's the power, then, that speech has to generate a jouissance that is jouissance of speech, and as a result, outside the body, but castrated. It is this structure that made it possible for me at the beginning of the year to comment on the phrase from Lacan that says that every formation, whatever it may be, consists in curbing jouissance. Yes, since every formation supposes speech, even if it flows from a neurobehavioral inspiration. Thus, the phallic function without the father. Incidentally, if you look at the construction of "L'étourdit", the function of the phallus is introduced before that of the father. Lacan reminds us of its function in the relation between the sexes and he says: an organ makes itself the signifier of analytic discourse because it is the discourses that create the organs as signifiers (c.f. appendicitis, foreskin, etc.). This organ "hollows out the place where the inexistence of the sexual relationship takes effect" (Lacan, 1973, p. 13). Lacan is going to insist quite a lot that it is at once the objection – it's jouissance is the one that shouldn't be, that of the idiot – and the supplement, which makes the relation possible. And the same goes for the propositional function. He says: "Hence a possible inscription (in the signification where the possible is foundational, Leibnizian) of this function as Φx to which beings are going to answer by means of their mode of making an argument here. This articulation of the function as proposition is that of Frege." Up to this point, no father.

Will it be said – by way of objection to this phallic function without the father but with speech – that speech, such as is advanced by Lacan, implies the father, as a signifier having the function of button tie for the entire edifice of language? This is what he had put forward at the time of the paternal metaphor, but in 1975, Lacan, having reworked his concept of the unconscious, also reworked his conception of speech. This is no longer the intersubjective speech of "The function and field of speech and of language", institutive of the partner, who said "you are my master" or "you are my wife". This full speech was indeed thought as being in solidarity with the function of the father, but then, Lacan noticed, as he says in the seminar *D'un discours qui ne serait pas du semblant*, that full speech is simply the speech that fills; and what would it fill other than the hole of the relationship which is lacking, just like the father-symptom? There where it is, this full-speech, it is no more than a cork, and fragile, because the non-relationship rather pushes towards a homophonic: "killed my wife [*tué ma femme*]" (Lacan, 1974, p. 61). More generally, in 1975, speech became, in Lacan's writing, the blah-blah, gabbing, chit chat, etc. It gleans no value from the button ties of signification, it enjoys [*se jouit*], and it is intrinsically a generator of the signification of the phallus. From here on, we notice, its relation to the father must be looked at again. Because, in fact, this overturning does not come from the seminar of 1975.

Over the years, Lacan regularly revisited what he called the *Bedeutung* of the phallus. It is the only complete genitive [*génitif complet*], he says in *D'un discours qui ne serait pas du semblant*, being objective and subjective, which means that it at once signifies and is itself a signified. Indeed, on the one hand, this phallus is the signifier that designates "the meaning effects [*effets de signifié*] as a whole, insofar as the signifier conditions them by its presence as signifier" (Lacan, [1958b] 2006, p. 579) (I have already mentioned this); but on the other hand, it is produced as signified because any chain of signifiers only ever signifies the phallus, that is to say castration, from the fact of its structure of pointing back, from signifier to signifier and from signification to signification – from the fact then of the impossibility of holding together all of the signifiers. In his Geneva conference, he specifies that signification was a bad translation of the *Bedeutung* of the phallus, which is in fact the "relationship to the real" (Lacan, 1985, p. 14). We are far from the imaginary. And which real? The one I have just mentioned, the impossibility of holding all of the signifiers together – this impossible whose name is castration. Because the latter is not the little story that we think it is but, if we trust "... ou pire", which dots the i's, castration is this impossibility itself. The speaking-being [*parlêtre*] is an "enjoys itself [*se jouit*]" – and, we should add, "for lack of a sexual relationship", unless we say as he does in the seminar *D'un discours qui ne serait pas du semblant*, that the sexual relationship is speech itself. In this speech, the father is not at all convoked. Speech is, starting with the seminar *Encore*, the place of the jouissance-unconscious. "The unconscious is the fact that being, in speaking, enjoys [*jouisse*]" (Lacan, 1999, pp. 104–105). More precisely, speech is the locus of the RUCS (real unconscious) inasmuch as it is a "spoken knowledge", and a knowledge is an enjoyed [*jouie*] *motérialité*, outside meaning, but which resides in the chains of speech. Some people quibble about the notion of the RUCS – so be it – but how could an enjoyed *motérialité*, coming from *lalangue*, be attributed to the symbolic? Let's move on.

From here on, the conception of the button tie itself must be rethought, which Lacan begins to do when at the end of *Encore*, he specifies that the One of the swarm of signifiers of language – those signifiers that are picked from the knowledge of *lalangue*, that are multiple, and that we thus decipher – the One of their set that Lacan names the master signifier, a new master signifier if I may say so, this One that "assures the unity of the subject's copulation with knowledge [...]", this incarnated One, "is not just any old signifier. It is the signifying order insofar as it is instituted on the basis of the envelopment by which the whole of the chain subsists" (Lacan, 1999, p. 143). Here is what is substituted for the father in order to insure the button-tying [*capitonnage*] of language.

The "*Y a d'l'Un*" includes it but is bigger. It contains yet another type of One than this master signifier, which he calls the One-saying [*Un-dire*], the One-saying that knows itself by itself on the side of the subject [*qui se sait tout seul côté sujet*]. The "*Y a d'l'Un*" is thus itself bifid, the One of the saying and the phallic One, which in analytic discourse is at the place of production. $/$S_1$. This is why Lacan formulates in "L'étourdit", speaking of the phallus, "that an organ makes itself the signifier of the analytic discourse" (Lacan, 1973, p. 12), and also that analytic discourse, that is to say an analysis, "puts the phallic function in its place" as function of castration, and this precisely by virtue of speech.

I said in passing that phallic jouissance is the one that we decipher, and we decipher it because it is ciphered by the unconscious. It's strange. For many years and without batting an eye, analysts have read in Lacan's writing the affirmation that the unconscious ciphers jouissance, but apparently, they had not, as a result, come to the conclusion of the RUCS, as outside meaning. However, the ciphering of jouissance is not of the symbolic. The two texts at the beginning of *Scilicet 5*, "... ou pire" and "L'introduction à l'édition allemande des *Écrits*", both written after "L'étourdit" and *Encore*, are very explicit on this point. You will read here that the *Arbeiter* that is the unconscious in its formations supposes a subject, and that the "jouissance that makes of the subject a function" is castrated (Lacan, 1975a, p. 9), this is his term. In the second text, it is even more clearly defined. The unconscious is "a knowledge of which it is only a question of deciphering because it consists in a ciphering" but, "in ciphering is sexual jouissance, certainly", and here is what stands in the way of the established sexual relationship (Lacan, 1975b, p. 14). We decipher it from speech, and when Lacan calls the unconscious a "spoken knowledge", it follows directly and logically from these developments.

And so, this phallic jouissance, which resides in speech, and which we decipher as a series of numbers, no one who speaks escapes it, if I may say so, and this makes it possible to shed light on various formulas from Lacan that could seem contradictory. An example: women, not-all in phallic jouissance, are not castratable. He repeats this in "... ou pire" and in *D'un discours qui ne serait pas du semblant*, and yet this does not prevent him from affirming that they have no more and no less castration than men – parity, for once. Is this contradictory? No. Insofar as they speak they fall under the castration effect of language, but at the level of sex, not having the organ that bears the castration effect of speech, their jouissance is possibly other, and this other jouissance is by definition not determined by speech. I could also call upon Joyce, or rather, *Lacan, lecteur de Joyce*, according to the title I have chosen for my next book, to be published at the beginning of 2015. In the knot that he draws in order to figure what he calls the lapsus of the knot for Joyce, real and symbolic are knotted. Phallic jouissance is here, unquestionably, in its place, the same as that of his epiphanies, according to Lacan. I conclude then: phallic jouissance, as castrated, is not an effect of the father.

The propositional function

However, when Lacan talks about the "propositional function", it is not simply phallic jouissance, nor even only the phallic function. He says it: there is "a possible inscription of the function of the phallus, a function that stands [*supplée*] in for the sexual relationship by being or having the phallus, as a proposition". Before "L'étourdit", the function was there, but not written as a proposition. "This articulation of the function as a proposition is that of Frege."

Frege reformalised the classical proposition, the grammatical one, as in the example *man is mortal*, subject, verb, complement. I am taking the example that Lacan uses at the beginning of "L'étourdit". He did it in extracting the verb. We can pose the function "to be mortal", which in itself is empty, but in which subjects can come to place themselves. We then say that they "make argument [*font argument*]" to the function. What does this change? It's that the propositional function does not predicate on the prior being of the subject. It does not bear any "you are [*tu es*]". It erases the metaphysical significance of the classical proposition because it is the proposition that determines the being of the subject so long as he comes to inscribe himself there, and not in a necessary way, and he inscribes himself here by a saying [*dire*]. It is so true that Lacan will be able to formulate from this the following year: they have a choice – although it is not the choice of their bodies. When we talk about the grammatical proposition, that is to say, of the syntax of statements [*énoncés*], we imply what every statement, every said [*dit*], supposes, namely, a saying [*dire*]. It is necessary to assess the change of perspective introduced by the "that one says" with which Lacan opens his text. This "that one says" puts the logic of language itself in suspense. With it, everything that can be formulated, that we attribute to the symbolic, where the logic of language indeed rules, is suspended to the act of enunciation, which does not fall within the scope of logic. Gödel's theorem showed it: a consistent system necessitates an element outside the system that incompletes it – and when I say necessity, it is logical necessity; there is no other necessity than logical necessity – but when the element in question is an existence of saying [*existence de dire*], we are no longer in the logic of language. We are in the contingency of discourse. There is no "universal that can be reduced to the possible", Lacan says, even death – which you could believe is real, because "all men are mortal" is a said [*dit*], and its universality dissimulates that it is said from somewhere, and from the place of the master. Lacan produces here an interpretation of the classical logic of the universal. Putting it in the form of a proposition allows him to bring the phallic function into this problematic of the only possible universal, and to bring in the father not as a signifier but as a saying [*dire*], which is indeed different. In order to pose a universal, a "for all [*pour tous*]", which also means for each one – each of the elements, amongst others, of the set of all – an exception that ex-sists is necessary. The logic of sets requires it. I will come back to this formula. This is what the two formulas of sexuation write.

The difference is clear. We do not say *every man is castrated*, which would be to validate an essence of man. It is not because he is man that he is inscribed in the castration function but because he is inscribed in it that he is man. Φx, the function produced by speech, is written on both sides of the formulas, precisely there where he puts psychosis. But in order to inscribe a phallic all, an exception that objects is necessary. For every $x\, \Phi x$ is thus only possible, not necessary. I said that the father of *Totem and Taboo* was an exception, but that of "L'étourdit" is not the same exception because for this exception, the function is neither true nor false. For the father of *Totem and Taboo* it was false: he escaped castration. And Lacan insists here that this exception makes no promise of a sexual relationship, as in the case of the *perorant outang* [perorating utang] possessing all of the women. He says precisely I quote, page 16, that this suspension of the function that objects to the relationship "is to the relationship only a means of access without hope".

We are miles away from any incarnation of the father, very far from the genitor, far even from any reference to coitus, or to he who had intercourse with the mother, far from convoking sex, and already this reduction to a logical necessity proper to language puts into question the subordination of the phallic function to what we commonly call the father, and even to a father as bearer of the father-function, which Lacan evokes in *R.S.I.* Indeed, this construction excludes that there be any saids, whatever they may be, proper to the father-function. The father is not a said of exception [*dit d'exception*] if he is the function of the saying of exception [*dire d'exception*], which, by definition, says nothing. His "*dire que non*" to all of the saids is a "beach [*plage*]", according to the term used by Lacan, where there are no saids. We can ask ourselves, why then equate this function of the exception with that of the Name-of-the-Father, who from the beginning – I mean, since Freud's Oedipus complex and since the paternal metaphor – was closely implicated in the question of sexual desire and reproduction. Is it only the weight of *lalangue* that justifies that one says that the saying is the father of all the saids? But why wouldn't we say the mother of all the saids?

Ex-sistence

Was I right to say the logic of sets requires it? Not exactly. I insisted on what Lacan says at the beginning of this text – it is psychoanalysis that elevates logic to the science of the real. We have an example with these formulas of the Oedipus complex. Indeed, the logic of sets deals with purely formal elements, which are not of the order of the saying. Lacan himself had, moreover, first of all situated the paternal exception not as a saying but as a formal element, a signifier that exsists to the set of signifiers, a minus-one, beginning with "The subversion of the subject and the dialectic of desire." The same goes for when he talks in *R.S.I.* of the symptom letter [*lettre symptôme*] that is identical to itself. It is an exception with respect to signifiers, as an element of the enjoyed unconscious [*inconscient joui*], but it is not a saying. There is thus a question about the status of what we call an existence. When Lacan writes it *ex-sistence*, in two words, it is in order to insist on the dimension of the topological place of the element in question. In a set, heterogeneous elements can be next to each other – we can mix dishcloths and napkins[1] – but in order for it to be a set, it is necessary that an element not belong to the set, not be included in it, not be an element of the set. And even if there are neither dishcloths nor napkins, even if it is Frege's empty set, it counts as one, a one that is not written in the set, that is not an element of the set, and which is another one [*un*] than the first of the whole numbers, which is zero. A minus-one is logically required in order to make a set, but what kind of minus-one? It is here that Lacan departs from the sole necessities of logic, because his One of exception is not a formal element, this one that speaks, that "*dit que non*" (says that no), and so ex-sistence is no longer only topological. It becomes an existence in the sense of presence. In the metaphor, we were dealing with a signifier, that is to say – Lacan himself formulated it – with the dead father. The father is the dead father, he said. It was an intuition of Freud's, with the murder of the father that Lacan reformulated as a father who was purely a signifier, independent of the presence of a flesh and blood father. Lacan did not use then the logic of sets, but the dead father, purely a signifier, went well with the purely logical exception. Only, there is a problem. We do not reproduce and we do not enjoy [*jouit*] by the operation of logic alone, and Lacan certainly noticed here that it didn't work for explaining the Oedipus complex of families, and as a result, he was concerned with the father who is in the bed, who didn't at all go with the dead father. Here, allow me to make a small digression. This distinction between the signifier and existence was present in "Remarks on Daniel Lagache's presentation", where after having situated all of the signifiers of structure, he notes at the beginning of part IV, entitled "Toward an ethics", that in order to introduce the superego, which he had set aside until then, it is necessary to take up things from the point of ... existence. "L'étourdit" introduces into the problematic a father, I don't dare to say a *living* father, but who is not the dead father, who is neither the father in the mother's bed, that's for sure, but who is a presence, one that responds. In "... ou pire", unless it is in *D'un discours qui ne serait pas du semblant*, you will find some developments on the phallus that say that the phallus never answers, and on the father who, on the other hand, responds. With the "that one says" with which Lacan opened his text – this "that one says" that designates the act of enunciation – we are outside of properly logical necessities, outside the sole implication of demonstrative systems. We are indeed at a level that convokes the exception, but an exception that is a saying, which is not reduced then to a logical implication, and which is posed as a contingency. I have said before that in Lacan's work, it was the "there is no such thing as a sexual relationship" that refuted the paternal metaphor, certainly, but it is necessary to add that this father who is not dead, but who isn't a body either, this saying-father[2] is another critical step beyond the metaphor for rethinking the experience differently and which clears the way for Lacan's final developments.

 R.S.I. added a development on fathers as people [*personnes pères*] who bear the function. This is the problem of what can give presence, even flesh, to the logical function. The father of *R.S.I.* (the lesson of January 21st), strangely resembles the classical father, who was indissociable from the conjugal couple of the family.

And we can seriously ask ourselves whether or not Lacan ever imagined what the evolution of society imposes today, that One father [*Un père*] can not only not have a specified sex, as is the case of that which names, but also not be the man of a woman-mother implied in reproduction. Does the father of the name, which he is going to add to the "*dire que non*" of the father, have a sex? The genitor is not the father, but the father as signifier or as name is always convoked in order to account for reproduction, which itself engages the questions of filiation. This is what the word father inevitably connotes. The metonymical extensions are not lacking in the common *lalangue*, as in father of the nation, little father of the peoples, but ... the motherland [*mère patrie*], etc.

Notes

1 [The French expression *mélanger les torchons et les serviettes*, to mix the dish cloths with the napkins, means to mix two things that do not belong together.]
2 [Here the French *père dire* indicates the father as a saying].

Chapter X
7th May 2014

Let me summarise what has already been said. In "L'étourdit", Lacan once again asked himself the Freudian question of what makes heterosexuality possible, it being understood that for those who speak, it cannot be a fact of nature. He must, as he says, obtain two halves corresponding to the *sex ratio*[1] of nature that conditions the survival of the species. He asks himself the question again after having advanced his "no such thing as a sexual relationship", no discourse of *suppléance* either, namely no sexual social link. The question is one of knowing if he succeeded in producing these two halves.

Two halves?
Lacan first of all put forward that the phallic all that makes what we call man implies the exception – logic requires it. But this exception, he conceives of it as a saying [*dire*], a "*dire que non*", and there, it is no longer logic that requires it. This ex-sistence is, I quote, the "subject supposed" (Lacan, 1973, p. 16) – let me emphasise *supposed* – to the suspension of the phallic function – which, let me remind you, is the function of castrated jouissance. From here on out, half of what we will call man is constituted. Which means, entirely [*tout*] in castrated jouissance, but also everyone [*tous*] in this jouissance. The exception founds the universal, and with it a universe, which we are going to call a masculine universe, composed of particulars who share in castration.

The other side differs. That a subject proposes itself to be called woman – notice the expression, it evokes a sort of project. It implies the double negation of the there *exists* – so, there does not ex-sist – and of the *for all* of the universal: it is not for all *x* that …, notations that Aristotle missed. I'm not going to go into this. I'll pause a moment on what Lacan names the logical power of the not-all [*pas-tout*]. The meaning of the saying which is inscribed from these quantifiers [*quanteurs*], he says, is that, of women (being not-all), "anything can be said [*tout puisse s'en dire*]", and he adds "even in arising from the reasonless [*même à provenir du sans raison*]". We would not say it for that which is *thomme*: the sense of the saying of the first two quantifiers is that, of men, not everything can be said (*tout ne peut pas s'en dire*); there is only one thing that can be said of them: all phallic jouissance, and not without reason, the reason being given by the name of the exception, of the "there ex-sists". As a result, if of women "anything can be said", it is in the sense of anything and everything, and which is certainly what happens. This field is opened by the reasonless, and it is an "outside-the-universe all [*tout d'hors univers*]", Lacan says. What is it? A multiplicity, necessarily, and which is not constituted as a set, in other words, a multiplicity that excludes the universal. Thus, two "alls [*tout*]", that of the universal conditioned by the exception, in which there are only particulars, in other words copies amongst other copies of the all in the phallic function. And then there is the outside-the-universe all, whose elements can only be singularities – singularities that can be taken one by one and that we count for lack of being able to homogenise them.

The formulas of sexuation escape classical logic and Lacan's references are to quantum logic. This logic, if I am not mistaken, is implicated in the very construction of the discourses. Lacan repeats very often, man and woman are signifiers. Yes, but signifiers are ordered by the discourses. These discourses, in Lacan's definition of them, imply the places of terms. The terms come from language. We know them, they apply to everyone, but where do the places come from? Lacan was much less explicit on this point. There is however an indication in "L'étourdit". Let me quote a phrase that appears essential to me, and which moreover is not totally comprehensible to me. He says, "There are two *dit-mensions*[2] of the for-all-man [*pourtouthomme*], that of the discourse from which he for-alls himself [*se pourtoute*] and that of the sites [*lieux*] from which it is this-manned [*ça se thomme*]" (Lacan, 1973, p. 16). Why this *t*? Because the question is one of knowing what makes man. The *t* writes the signifying sonority. Analytic discourse proceeds from this second *dit-mension*, Lacan says, that of the places then. He comes to write, the father makes "a site of his beach [*lieu de sa plage*]". The beach is the space where the phallic function is in suspense. We could go on and on about this image of the beach, link it to this other image of Lacan, that of the coastline [*littoral*] that he used in *Lituraterre* and which separates the two domains of the fluidity of oceans and of terrestrial reliefs. Let's move on. The thesis is that the places [*places*] that constitute the discourses – named here, I think, the sites [*lieux*] – depend on the exception, and a site is necessary for the semblant to be able to come to it, and even various semblants according to the various discourses. The thesis is coherent with the notion of psychosis as outside discourse if the structure of discourse depends on the father as a logical exception. Lacan defined the places at the end of "Radiophonie": the place of the agent, a site to which a semblant will come; the place of truth; the place of the other, who is other than the agent who makes a couple with him; and the place of production. In order to situate "the sites of *thommage*" from which psychoanalysis proceeds, Lacan takes up the four places designated in "Radiophonie". The sites are identifiable from their making "sense of the semblant". I explained how the meaning of a discourse comes from the semblant at the place of the agent – the semblant here being the phallus. And then, from the truth that there is no such thing as a sexual relationship because of the phallus – a unique semblant. And then, a jouissance that stands in [*y supplée*] at the place of the other – who is other than the semblant – phallic jouissance. And then, from the product, the surplus jouissance [*plus-de-jouir*].

As an aside: what is interesting is that Lacan introduced the phallus as Freud does, starting with those to whom, I quote, "biological heritage is generous with the semblant", an indication that I am lingering on because it indicates the anchoring of this major semblant of sex, the phallus, in the biological real. There are many other indications from Lacan that are in line with this. The *sex ratio* is, moreover, not a fact of language. Obviously, if this semblant comes from biological heritage, it is not ready to disappear and does not depend on the father. What depends on it is its coming to the place of the semblant.

For the bearer of the semblant, the sites of this *thommage* are an *a priori* damage [*dommage*]. The damage, obviously, can only be that of castration. The sites preside over the inevitability of castration. *A priori* damage, this means that it doesn't owe anything to history, only to structure. On it is also grafted the *a posteriori* of the discourses – of the common discourse transmitted by the saying of the parents, who would like to educate the organ in order to make a man, a real one.

The *for-all-man* is thus not biological, despite the *sex ratio*. And if it is a race, that of men, it is like every race, an effect of art. It is constituted, I quote, "from the mode from which is transmitted, through the order of a discourse, the symbolic places, those from which is perpetuated the race of the masters, no less than that of the slaves, and of the pedants as well, and, in order to answer for them, some *pédés* [ped-ed, or pederasts], some *scients* [knowers, or those who are scient] are necessary, I might add, so that it not go without some *sciés* [who are stunned, or sawed]" (Lacan, 1973, p. 19).[3] We are here in the historical register, where the places are occupied by different semblants according to the discourses of the time, and in no way do the signifiers man and woman figure here.

There are several questions to ask regarding this translation of the *sex ratio* into two logical halves, all and not-all. And first of all, did Lacan succeed in obtaining two halves that reduplicate the *sex ratio* that would be necessary for ensuring the continuation of the species? One might well doubt it. "L'étourdit" certainly puts forward that, for want of a sexual relationship, the logical exception of the father is the condition of man, a condition, then, so that those who speak are divided into two halves corresponding to those of the *sex ratio*. In other words, the father remains the condition of heterosexuality, but it is not a sufficient condition. If they have a choice of being on one side or the other, regardless of anatomy, then the two halves, all and not-all, have no reason to correspond to the *sex ratio*. If they have a choice, this reduplication does not arise from any logical necessity. It is only possible, and nothing guarantees that the two halves are going to continue to be based on the *sex ratio*. I have mentioned, moreover, that Tiresias, after the punishment of becoming a woman, still chooses to become a man again. They have a choice, Lacan formulated it the following year, notably for mystics and for the hysteric, but the thesis is there starting with "L'étourdit". When he says a subject *proposes* to be called woman. And when we isolate all of the passages consecrated specifically to women in "L'étourdit", what do we see?

To say it in a condensed form, he recognises their right – the expression being "I don't require them" – the right to "withdraw" themselves [*se retrancher*] from the phallus. He even attributes to the not-all [*pas-toute*], that claims not to recognise itself in those who enter into the dance of discourse, the perception of the structure of the places that he constructed and which, with phallic jouissance and surplus jouissance, forecloses the Other, the Other of sex (Lacan, 1973, p. 24). He even says that he worries that the MLF, which was a current topic at the time, would only be a flash in the pan. In short, he pleads for the Other, as a jouissance that does not fall under the phallic One, and for the singularity of women, whom nothing obliges to enter into the discourse that *for-alls* subjects. I am using here the verb *for-all* [*pourtouter*], created by Lacan in order to designate the operation of each discourse. But for the other logic, it would be difficult to use the verb *for-not-all* [*pourpastouter*], since it does not make any all.

Various not-alls

The logic of the not-all covers a broad spectrum, but it is to be distinguished from what "inhabits it" – this is Lacan's term – in other words, from that to which it is applied as jouissance, since logic is in itself as empty as an axiom. When it comes to women, what inhabits the not-all jouissance is the other jouissance. What about when it is a question of psychotics, who Lacan puts under the same logic and who he also says are "outside discourse", something that he does not say about women? And then there are the mystics. Lacan denies that it is a question of "cum stories [*histoires de foutre*]", as ordinary bawdiness would have it. As for today's psychoanalysts, they readily suspect the mystics of psychosis, even though the mystics were not outside discourse, far from it. They were sustained by an entire discourse, even when suspected of heresy. One still must add to this series the analyst who also comes under the logic of the not-all, and not of the One of the father. This is why Lacan avoids saying The Analyst [*L'analyste*] as much as Woman [*La femme*].

The not-all of psychosis

Lacan puts psychosis on the side of the not-all, a question that extends into that of the madness of women, and he goes so far as to say that his discourse "can even be shown to be grounded in psychosis" (Lacan, 1973, p. 51).[4]

If psychosis is placed on the side where the exception is lacking, we must say of it what Lacan says for women: anything can be said about psychotics, in the way I have just mentioned. Note that this is not the way that psychiatry has chosen, which in its best periods, the classical ones, employed itself in making drawers, by which I mean categories. The psychiatrist adheres as though by nature to the logical categories of Aristotle, with the hope no doubt of reducing the case-by-case that would correspond to the one-by-one of women. Look at what they squeezed into the schizophrenia drawer for example, so long as the systematic delusion of paranoia (another drawer) is lacking: Artaud, Joyce, but also the entire range of chronic aboulics, foreign to any social link. What I am calling drawers is at the level of thought, but if you reread "Le savoir du psychanalyste", the conferences given by Lacan at Sainte-Anne in 1970, where he says, "I speak to the walls [*Je parle aux murs*]" from which Miller created a title that erases the title chosen by Lacan, "Le savoir du psychanalyste"! He said, I speak to the walls, after having heavily insisted that he had come to speak to psychiatrists; you will see that what he points out – and this is incidentally only an aspect of these conferences – is that the drawers of thought are reinforced, even found themselves, with other walls – not to be confused with the wall of language – those of the asylum that are indeed necessary for what he clearly designates as … the segregation of mental illness. This was not an ode to the psychiatrist, contrary to what people sometimes say. It is in psychosis that Lacan was interested, and he only speaks to the psychiatrist in order to rectify his position precisely with respect to psychosis. Moreover, let us not forget that the unconscious was discovered by a non-psychiatrist and that the trajectory of Lacan, who had all of the tools of psychiatry in hand, led him to psychoanalysis, and that when he speaks to psychiatrists, it is never to praise them. His praises are for psychosis itself and for the psychoanalyst. There is only one text of praise, "British psychiatry and the war", but if he sings the praises of psychiatrists, it is not for their treatment of psychosis, but for having worked so efficiently for the constitution of the army that England was lacking. Whatever the case, there is no more universal of Psychosis [*La psychose*] than of Woman [*La femme*].

In any case, all of Lacan's points are coherent, starting with the notion of psychosis as outside discourse. This is logical if the places depend on the exception. As a result, because of the *a priori* damage that Lacan diagnosed for he who calls himself man, one would be wrong to think that psychosis necessarily designates a handicap. It would rather be outside of damage. And what is the function of this damage, which has for its name, I have said, castration? It is quite ambiguous. On the one hand, it oversees, certainly, so that it is possible to "make love" to a partner, a partner elevated to the signifier of the phallus. Without it, Lacan says, there is no means of making love to the partner, even if we do all kinds of things to him that resemble it a great deal. But on the other hand, it is this damage of castration that generates all of the inhibitions and impotencies, not only in the domain of love but also in that of work. Outside of damage then, the psychotic, to quote Lacan, "enters as a master in the city of discourse".[5] He is the free man, he said early on, which means, among other things, free from *a priori* damage, but also not chained to the *a posteriori* order of the symbolic places of discourse. And it is just as true of the one who I called aboulic, outside any link, as it is of subjects of exception who subvert the *a posteriori* of discourses. As a result, from one end to the other of the spectrum of the psychoses, anything can be said, first one thing and then its opposite. No universal, but rather the logic of the not-all.

I'll pause here to comment on what Lacan diagnosed in the Schreber case as "push-to-woman [*pousse-à-la-femme*]". In "L'étourdit" he insists and specifies that it is the effect of the first quantifier: there does not exist any "*dire que non*" to the phallic function. From then on, the subject has no choice. He cannot place himself on the all-phallic side, in spite of his penis. But how is his push-to-woman realised? We can see it with Schreber, in the imaginary, through images of the woman – the chest with breasts contemplated at the mirror – in the symbolic, through the God-wife that he becomes – through the mother of a future humanity that he promises to be – and in the real, through the exquisite pleasure of which he speaks. The push-to-woman is a solution. Why? Because the signifier of woman is supposed to make up [*suppléer*] for the signifier of the Other's lack, the phallus, and allows the subject an identification of *suppléance*. Let me remind you that the primary function of the phallus in Lacan's construction is to allow the subject the identification of his living being [*être de vivant*]. Lacan pointed out with subtleness that if Schreber was able to accept this solution, it is because he had died beforehand. He had seen his death announced in the newspaper. Having taken on the image of woman, he resurrects in some ways as a woman. This signifier breathes life back into him in the relation to the Other.

A few years later, Lacan proposes another formula for paranoia. It "identifies jouissance in the place of the Other" (in the introduction to the translation of *Memoirs of my Nervous Illness*). One must not think that this signifies simply that, as in the delusion of persecution, it is the partner who enjoys, whether he is divine or human. It is the same with the postulate of the neurotic fantasy. "Identifying jouissance in the place of the Other." It has to be taken literally. It consists in equating jouissance with the signifier, jouissance and words of which the Other is made. Schreber's god is an infinite text, he specifies this, and Schreber is a part of this text. The proof is in the interrupted phrases that he must complete and above all in the bellowing-miracle, the subjective shredding when God withdraws. There is here a modality, rising from the text, of this coalescence of thought and jouissance that Lacan makes explicit starting with *Encore*. Indeed, in Schreber's delusion, God is the sum total of everything that has been thought since the beginning of time by all of the deceased souls. In other words, the sum of all of the elements, of all of the *lalangues*. Except that this text of the dead must be revivified, jouissance must be restored to it, which is what Schreber does.

Here then is the phallic jouissance of the psychotic, which is the jouissance of words, but with a difference: not words from his unconscious in particular, but from all of *lalangue*. The jouissance of the couple that he forms with God overwhelms the entire space of *lalangue*, and with this ubiquity of phallic jouissance, the transition to Joyce would be easy if not for the delusion.

The delusion poses the problem of the relationship to reality, and the father is implicated here. Lacan says: the "real of this beach", that of the father then, "realises the relationship of which the semblant is the supplement". In other words, when the phallic semblant comes to this place, this beach, it stands in [*supplée*] for the relationship. Let me rephrase, the real of this beach realises the relationship. This is its function at the level of sex, but, I cite, it is only fantasy, namely the relationship of $\bar{S}$ with the *objet petit a* of his fantasy; the fantasy, Lacan continues, that "supports all of our reality, as given by all of the five senses". Without the phallus as S_1 that has come to the real of this beach, the relationship to reality is affected as much as the relationship to sex is. In other texts, Lacan formulated, "reality is fantasy", it is constituted from the object *a*. Lacan takes up here his initial idea, of a father who is at the basis of the adjustment not only of sex by the phallus at the place of the semblant, but also of the link to reality by the fantasy, except that it is no longer a question of the father of the oedipal family with his norms, but of the existential logical exception without norms. There where this father commands, it is logic that commands, as in the analytic act, and there where the father does not command, it is another logic that commands, failing which, analytic discourse could not be applied to psychosis.

The not-all of women

For women, the question has long been asked: are they crazy? Not crazy at all [*pas folles du tout*],[6] Lacan says in *Television*, but there are some who all the same are on the side of psychosis. Everything hangs on the "there does not exist an *x* such that not phi of *x*", which is the new writing of foreclosure.

Let me note, before entering further into this question, that women's relationship to reality was called into question almost more than their relationship to sex: first of all, in the "all women are crazy" – which Lacan rejects – but also by Freud himself. For the jouissance of women, he throws in the towel [*donne sa langue au chat*], the dark continent, but for reality – which moreover according to him supposes a desexualisation running contrary to Lacan's thesis – he is categorical: there is a feminine deficiency. The theme would be worth following closely. It is in agreement with the common, popular theme of a plus of subjectivity in women and thus a minus of objectivity, Freud's construction being that only libido – and libido is male – supports the relationship to reality. In our terms, we also say that it is phallic jouissance that supports it. Lacan often came back to this to prevent any misunderstandings – women have no less of a relationship to phallic jouissance than do men – explicitly denouncing a so-called anti-phallic nature that some people wanted to read into his formulas. If women are here not-all, neither are they here not at all.

Where is the difference? Given that she doesn't have the organ, a woman can hardly hope to see herself being attributed the phallus. Here, let's not forget that Schreber, staying with his example, is not, as Lacan says, "foreclosed from the penis". What goes wrong with Schreber is precisely the attribution of a phallus to his person, and even more than that, to males in general, for want of the first two formulas; for him, there are no men, which is not the case for most women – this is the difference. However, to attribute a phallus is to attribute castration, hence

Lacan's phrase that says that it is castration that is transmitted from father to son as well as his remarks that a woman is not castratable. Indeed, only those whose penis can be elevated to the phallic semblant, if I may say so, are castratable. Lacan says that "biological heritage is generous with the semblant" to the male half, but the semblant does not come from biological heritage. Who can attribute it? The saying of the parents, which certainly targets the organ? One could think so, but no, that is not the thesis of "L'étourdit" because the saying of the parents is only *a posteriori*. The condition of a possible attribution is *a priori*. It is in the logical exception, without which, as is the case for Schreber, there would be no men. When there are some, a woman can distinguish herself from them, but nothing obliges her, since those who speak have a choice, and Lacan often pointed out the ease with which women play the man [*faire l'homme*]. If she distinguishes herself from him, instead of playing the man, she can be the phallus and even the "sublime phallus that guides man towards his true layer, which in following his route, he lost", Lacan says (Lacan, 1973, pp. 24–25).[7] Indeed, it is not the route of nature that guides him towards the layer of the other half, but only the semblant. The sublime phallus is a place holder of the *Woman* [*La femme*] who doesn't exist.

A not-all society?

We can also ask: what logic does the society of contemporary, financial capitalism obey? Capitalism is in solidarity with the requirement of parity. Capitalism did not engender disparity – whether at the sexual level or at the level of the organisation of labour – it inherited it. We must specify though that parity is not to be completely confused with the ideal of an equality of rights, although it in fact follows it. All of the discourses that have been indexed as linking structures [*structures de lien*] are characterised by disparity. I insisted on this last year. They consist of a semblant in the place of command and its other that is commanded by it. As a result of this, there is a contradiction between the requirement of a social link, at least in Lacan's view, and the requirement of parity. Additionally, the discourses are not sympathetic with one another. Lacan evoked the "racism of discourses in action", which signifies that each prefers his modes of jouissance to those of the Other, and on this matter moreover, so-called machismo is not a simple racism: it is not that it simply prefers its jouissance, it's that it attempts to eliminate the Other. It is an attempt at foreclosure. This goes well with what Lacan says: "There is no woman but the one excluded by the nature of things, which is the nature of words." There is a paradox here of egalitarian demands for women, which consist in making women citizens like everyone else, citizens made equal by the same discourse, whereas by definition, as Other, discourse excludes them. Citizens like everyone else they may be, but then, they are not here, specifically as women, Other. It is from there that we must consider Lacan's remark, which is shocking in some respects, when he says that Marx was wrong on one point – that of pushing women to fight for equality.

In capitalism, the current disruption of symbolic hierarchies that we attribute to the long-term effects of science has become obvious. It manifests itself everywhere, even in families in the triumph of individualism, threats on pyramidal organisations, the rise of more or less egalitarian [*paritaire*] collectives that I named aggregates, so-called social networks, etc., and in all of these reworkings of what some people call *hyper-modernity*, to which we bear witness without knowing how far they will go. They signal, more than the decline of the father of the family of which so much is said, the disappearance of the constitutive places of Lacan's four discourses. As a result, when Lacan tries to write the structure of a capitalist discourse at one point in Italy, we see right away that it is not properly speaking a discourse. He writes the four terms, S_1, S_2, $\bcancel{S}$ and a, implicated by language, but the places with their specificities, without which there is no discourse-link, are no longer there. I have often said in the writing of the capitalist discourse: from the subject who commands the symbolic (S_1, S_2), in order to produce the surplus jouissances, which command the subject, there is a circle, even a vicious one, the only link being that of the subject to its jouissance.

$$\frac{\bcancel{S}}{S_1} \downarrow \bcancel{\times} \downarrow \frac{S_2}{a}$$

This thesis is coherent with the one in "L'étourdit", according to which the constitutive places are a function of the father exception that "makes a site of his beach". Accordingly, without the disparity of the places, there is no *for-all* men, but a regime that seems to apply itself to *for-not-alling* rather than to *for-alling*, and ultimately to producing what Lacan named "scattered, ill-matched individuals", "unarities". In fact, Lacan says it while considering the modalities of jouissance that produce for each subject his unconscious; capitalism produces it by reducing each to being the object of the mercantile machine, as producer/consumer. The question being how from here on, these ones can at some point assemble themselves. It is from this that the protest of women is best justified: because if they are all objects of the machine, they might as well be equal, and when Lacan denounces this demand [*revendication*] he does not place himself in this register of capitalisation but in that of sexuation.

Notes

1 [In English in the original].
2 [The writing *dit-mension* introduces the word *dit* [said] into the word "dimension".]
3 [Lacan seems to be making several wordplays here. *Pédants* [pedants], goes with *pédés*, which commonly means "queers" or "pederasts" in French. Although both words actually exist in French, Lacan seems to be using *pédants* and *pédés* as present and past participles, both used substantively, of an invented French verb, which we could write *péder*. Thus, *pédants* and *pédés* would refer, respectively, to those carrying out the action of the non-existent verb *péder* and to those receiving the action of the verb. *Scient* are those who know, who are actively knowing, and *sciés*, the substantive

form of the past participle of the verb *scier* (to saw, or even to astound), would seem to indicate those who are receiving the action of the *scients*: *Elle se constitue du mode dont se transmettent par l'ordre d'un discours les places symboliques, celles dont se perpétue la race des maîtres et pas moins des esclaves, des pédants aussi bien, à quoi il faut pour en répondre des pédés, des scients, dirai-je encore à ce qu'ils n'aillent pas sans des sciés.*]

4 [*"se démontre pouvoir se soutenir même de la psychose"*].
5 See the report on *La logique du fantasme* (Lacan, 1984a).
6 [This could also be translated as: "Not crazy about the all".]
7 [*"phallus sublime qui guide l'homme vers sa vraie couche, de ce que sa route, il l'ait perdue"*]

Chapter XI
21st May 2014

"L'étourdit", which I have spent a lot of time on, is not the end of Lacan's developments regarding the paternal function. It is only a step. In *R.S.I.*, Lacan defines *a* father who is the bearer of the function, and he then introduces, no longer the father as bearer of the function who "*dit que non* [says that no]", a formula from "L'étourdit", but the father of the name, defined by the saying of naming [*dire de nomination*], and this is essentially his last development.

A father

Allow me to pause once more on this page dedicated to a father in the lesson of January 21st 1975. He is defined in two ways: by his symptom and by his saying. The symptom is the relation that stands in [*supplée*] for the non-relationship, and in this case, it is a woman, the cause of desire and the mother of children. It is a classic symptom, I said. Lacan is obviously talking about the father of the oedipal family here. As for his saying, it must be only a half-saying, the half-saying of his truth, of the truth of his desire and of his jouissance. Why? The saying [*dire*] makes for a God-saying [*dieu-re*], Lacan says. Indeed, the saying poses and supposes an *ex-sistence*, and God is saying. The father shouldn't be God then, but rather a half-God-saying [*mi-dieure*]. Again, I ask: what necessitates this just-right suppression of the symptom of *suppléance* for the relationship that is his? I have come to think that it is linked to the fact that the father gives rise to identification – and this thesis indicates, in my opinion, without formulating it explicitly – with what of the father it is better to identify. It is not the same thing to get one's bearings on desire as it is to get one's bearings on jouissance. The advantage of identification with desire, about which Lacan made a big deal in the beginning and above all with respect to hysteria, is that we don't know what desire wants. It leaves room for interpretation, which Lacan writes as the x of an unknown. The half-saying [*mi-dire*] of the father, precisely because it does not say all, is favourable to it. On the contrary, when desire is very or too determined, too readable, or too obvious [*cousu de fil blanc*], when the x of its enigma is covered over for lack of a half-saying, for lack of only being said between the lines, in veiled terms as we say, it is as though the signifying interval were clogged, and so the discourse of the father becomes holophrased, which is favourable for producing psychotic effects. From this comes specifically what Helene Deutsch called "as if" personalities, as well as those patients who obviously feel persecuted. This is how I explain to myself the psychoses that are so frequent in the children of those whom we call great men, geniuses of writing, of politics, or of science. Think of Victor Hugo, Joyce, Einstein, and many others, who are all cases of desire that is so decided, so constant, so unique that it takes the form of a vocation, and leaving very little room for the half-saying, leaves none for interpretation and makes for a God-saying [*dieu-re*]. We often come to the conclusion of their psychoses but without further explanation.

The father of the name

Let me turn now to the father of the name, to the saying that names. I have already mentioned that if the father is a saying, whatever this saying may be, he is not, cannot be, a dead father, a simple signifier. We are beyond the father of the oedipal metaphor of the signifier about which we could have believed that it was transported by the desire of the mother. This is why, starting with "L'étourdit", Lacan looks for the mainspring of foreclosure on the side of the father instead. A saying is not a living breeder [*reproducteur*] either. Hence the question that I evoked: why name what names father? We must suppose that there is in naming a power of generation, of engendering, but which one?

It is distinguished from the simple engendering of bodies that are necessary for the survival of the species. The father is not the genitor. This is an unchanging thesis of Lacan's. For the father of "L'étourdit", the logical exception of the saying "*dit que non* [says that no]" to the phallic function but took part all the same in the sexuation of the two halves and was thus essential for the reproduction of bodies. Lacan evokes this at several points in his text. I have insisted on this. But for the father who names, we can ask ourselves if what names has some relationship to sex and if it has a necessary function in the sexuation of those who speak. In any case, at the time of the Borromean knot, the question of sexuation is no longer central, even when Lacan is wondering about the couple, about what knots, he presupposes sexuation. And we also have to ask, "What is named?" because many things can be named.

Every saying is an exception with respect to what is said. Every saying as such is a "*dire que non*" that ex-sists to the saids of truth. The saying envelops the language of truth, but it also puts it in suspense. This relationship of the saying to the saids that Lacan introduced in "L'étourdit", is it also applicable to the saying of naming? Yes, since we can distinguish the saids of names, these saids that attribute a name to a referent – this is what happens in the Garden of Eden – and the fact that these saids of names do not go without a saying that ex-sists to them. Naming as an act and saids of names are to be distinguished. When Lacan talks about the father of the name, it is a question of the father as a saying. The saying of naming is also excepted from all of the saids of names. It is an act that ex-sists to these saids. This is so true that we can rechristen a referent and re-baptise it, that is, change the name according to a new saying. This is because between the name and its referent, namely what is named, there is no relationship. Arbitrariness of the name. It is not the signifier that is arbitrary with respect to the signified, as Saussure said. It is the name that is arbitrary with respect to its referent. So, what then is the specificity of the saying of naming since all of the sayings are not sayings of naming, and since the function of names is distinguishable from the function of naming?

The big difference between signifier and name is that the first produces some signified and misses the referent, the referent that is in the place of the real in the field of language. The name, on the contrary, hangs onto, or hooks, a referent. It pins it, but it has no signified. In the Biblical myth, creation precedes naming [*nomination*]. The creatures of God are there as so many referents before they are given a name. These creatures themselves are the product of a saying, a *God-saying*: let there be light, and there was light. In the beginning was the word, but the word is not the signifier – it's the saying, here the generating saying. In the Bible, the saying of creation, *ex nihilo*, precedes the saying of naming [*dire de nomination*], which comes after it. And the name attributed is essentially arbitrary with respect to the creature. Why is the horse called *horse* rather than *tatata*? Will we say that *horse* is the name of a species, a common name then? In the Babel of languages, what is proper to the common name is that it is translatable, which is not the case of the proper name. Only the Bible tells us that common names, *horse* for example, were initially proper names stapled on to *an* original creature, the ancestor of each species. The name of the species would thus be, in some ways, some proper name that turned into the common name because of reproduction or perpetuation. Obviously, when these are beings that do not speak, that are named, naming is performative – I have already said this – because they don't talk back. Once named *horse*, this creature and his offspring will from here on out be called horse. But we can say about this what Lacan says at the beginning of *Television* concerning animals: "They only have being from being named." This is a way of saying that the name makes be [*fait être*], or that being only has meaning within the language of naming. If the name is generating, it engenders, not simple existence, but being.

The function of the name

We can see the difference between the naming of the horse and the naming of someone who speaks: the latter has the power to talk back, as he can accept or reject the name that is given, according to whether he will perceive it more as something imposed, or on the other hand, as a gift, even a grace. Practices of name changing exist and would be worth questioning. I have already insisted on this: the name is always placed in a social link – there is no self-naming – and so we can ask, "What is rejected when a subject rejects his name?" But on the other hand, what does he gain when he accepts it or when he renames it? In any case, these practices indicate, beyond a shadow of a doubt, that there is a subjective significance of the name and, as a result, of its absence. We see this especially with the names received from the register of births, deaths, and marriages [*état civil*], the names of genealogy, and also what the twists and turns of life potentially bring to this name.

The names that we receive, to be differentiated from those that we make for ourselves, can come from different sources. From love, certainly: these are often intimate names, Lacan evoked this very early on, and I illustrated it myself with Claudel's Ysé in *Break of Noon*, but ultimately it is only theatre – and perhaps it is also a thing of the past. In any case, these are precarious names, outside of the theatre. It is, however, the case that in genealogical transmission, love is not without having a role. In certain circumstances, the position of a subject with respect to the name received and with respect to the saying of transmission of the name are easily distinguishable. This is the case when the name, being either obscene or suggestive, is recused without it seeming to implicate the relationship to the saying of transmission. But there are also subjects who keep impossible names, socially impossible ones, out of consideration for this saying of transmission. Essentially, the relationship of a subject to his name is a sign: the sign of his more or less unreconciled relationship to the Other, specifically to what Lacan named the "traumatic parent", in the sense that I indicated previously, and in which, whatever the affects may be, each subject remains rooted. Perhaps this is what Freud was aiming at when he spoke of this well-known primordial identification with the father, so primordial that it remains out of the reach of the clinic.

Let me turn now to the name that is made by means of various works, the names of notoriety. The name of glory, even of vainglory, or the name of infamy. In every case they are placed in genealogy, as Lacan says in the "Italian note." Only, we must not forget – he emphasised this – that serving genealogy is not the way of the psychoanalyst, who is not supposed to work for the ancestor, in other words for God the father. Making a name for oneself is precisely the undertaking of what in the end Lacan names "making for oneself a stepladder": it elevates your name. Without the name, your merits would not be. They would be, in any case, without profit for you because they would not be inscribed in universal memory, at least the one we like to imagine as universal. This is what happens for the Saint if we believe the second conference on Joyce, because the saint does not look to be a saint. There is no saint but in the renouncing of sainthood; the saint undergoes "*scabeaustration*", "the castration of the stepladder [*escabeau*]" (Lacan, 1979, p. 33). In other words, the saint, if he is one, does not want a saint name for himself. When in *Television*, Lacan establishes a homology between the status of the Saint and that of the analyst, that's what it means. For both of them there is "*scabeaustration*", the elision of the name, except that for the saints, those of the church, there is a little posthumous compensation: we canonise them. This is not the case of the analyst as such – to be distinguished from the actual person – which is why, concerning the analytic act, I spoke of an act "without remuneration". Moreover, let us notice, it is amusing, that a History of psychoanalysis, with a capital H since this has been attempted, is essentially a history of the names of authors of analytic theory. For the others, those who have not written then, it is very difficult to write their History in the sense of a scientific discipline, and especially the discipline of sources, because what remains of them is only what the *vox populi* of a thousand voices says of them, which is essentially the rumour of the opinions of contemporaries. And so, more amusing still is that for some, the so-called history greatly resembles a kind of lay canonisation that raises a few proper names, raises them in making for them a posthumous stepladder, and the agent of this canonisation is not the Pope, but the author who writes this history without a capital H. From this is also possibly clarified the frenzy of publications that has gripped analysts since the end of the École Freudienne. Lacan tried to contain it with *Scilicet* and the project of unsigned works, which indicates that he saw it coming, but in vain. All of this nevertheless shows very well that most often, it is also necessary to receive the name that one makes for oneself, and many fret about how to achieve it. Especially since the number of publications makes it all the more perceptible that their destination is … the garbage can, the garbage can of forgetfulness, the hole that swallows up the Babel of discourses.

The function of naming

I wonder about the specificity of the saying of naming, the one that gives the name. Lacan situated it in the Borromean knot, and it occurred to me that the saying of naming could very well be a "*dire que oui*" (saying that yes). But yes to what? When it comes to naming that which doesn't speak, it is a yes to an existing referent that it shifts into being, and which only has being from being named. But it is also guaranteed for the naming that comes from love, whether it is sexed or parental love. Is it not, moreover, what the final pages of *Encore* say, which make of love an obscure recognition of the position of the partner relative to his destiny as one who speaks, to the destiny that his unconscious makes for him? To name [*nommer*] is "*dire que oui*" – not to be confused with qualifying. Naming does not qualify, it does not predicate, as insulting does. It says yes to a referent of encounter. In this case, to name [*nommer*] is to give the gift of being. This is what certain logicians do. Lacan evokes Bertrand Russell, and he seems to designate it as a naming of the imaginary because it can only take the body as referent. It is not the case of every naming. In constructing the formulas of sexuation and the discourses, Lacan, I have reminded you, finds his bearings in the logic called quantum logic [*quantique*], the logic that reworks the modalities of classical logic, and he situates the saying in general here as the *a priori* condition of the four places and terms, in other words, as a real. But the saying of naming, in the strong sense, in its specificity, does it not rather come from a modality that I'll call *cantique*, written with a c, as in the name of Cantor, who resolves the transfinite of whole numbers by a saying that creates the name of the first aleph-zero? It is not the saying of an additional number. In this sense, like every saying, it ex-sists to the series of whole numbers, but it is *dire que oui* in the sense that, in acknowledging an impossible, it adds to it, through the saying, the creation of a new number that is going to make the handling of it possible. This saying is a real that is not only existential, that cannot be demonstrated, that appears – emergence, epiphany, if you wish – but that also functions as the origin of a new mathematical language. Such a production is a beginning, which is why Lacan says "discourse of mathematics" and not language of mathematics – discourse, because the said is here renewed by the saying. It is no longer as in the Bible. The distinction that I made between the saying that produces the creatures and the saying that names them, and which came second, disappeared – to name [*nommer*] and to create are here one and the same act. In the case of Cantor, the saying of the name of the aleph-zero is more than naming something that exists – it is engendering.

Lacan made a parallel between the saying of mathematics and the saying of analysis, insofar as the saids, the saids that have come from the unconscious, are here renewed by the saying. He even applied this to his own person, saying that in producing the triad of the three names S, I, R, he succeeded in elevating his own name. The common names S, I, R were already in *lalangue*, certainly, but not as solid substantives, solid enough that we can now say the Imaginary, the Symbolic, and the Real. And Lacan comments that producing names or some new name, elevates your own name. That was just a small remark that indicates all the same that the stepladder of the proper name doesn't only have one step, if I may say so. Producing a name is a step, but not the only one. One wouldn't say for example of Joyce that he produced new names, rather the opposite. Although he did indeed elevate his own.

On this question of the production of the name, I cannot not evoke this passage that I put on hold in my previous lessons, a difficult passage where Lacan talks about the hole of the symbolic. Moreover, he said about this hole, in response to a question, that it is what he named the Thing, *das Ding*, the real inasmuch as it suffers [*pâtit*] from the signifier according to *The Ethics of Psychoanalysis*. At the time of the Borromean knot, he specifies that a hole swallows up but also spits out – and what does it spit out? Names-of-the-Father. This is his lesson of April 25th in *R.S.I*. The Freudian name of the hole is "primal repression". This hole swallows up, in effect, because the Thing, the Freudian Thing is ... the unnameable. In our language, this term is equivocal. He adds to its major signification the absence of any possible name, a nuance of repulsive affect, the expression "It's unnameable", always carrying a nuance of disapproval. But the unnameable is not the real outside the symbolic, because it does not demand anything from anybody and does not aspire to be named. The unnameable only has meaning in the field where one aspires to a naming, that is, within the function of speech. Here the unnameable designates a limit, that of language. The cry of the Thing is "I, truth, am speaking"; I am speaking, but I remain out of reach. Primal repression, says Freud. The Thing is this unnameable that the half-said of truth at once manifests and misses. As a result, the unnameable is thus not only what speaks. It also produces what I can call a push-to-naming [*pousse à la nomination*].

The unnameable is what does not pass through the signifier. It is, then, never represented in the Other and is precisely at the place of the hole in the Other. Before speaking about the hole in the symbolic, Lacan, in "The subversion of the subject and the dialectic of desire", when he was constructing his graph of desire, formulated the question posed by the subject about his identity: what am I? He responded: I am at the place of jouissance, this place that he wrote S(A), and he made of it nothing less than the generator of the proper name. This is already a way of saying that that which cannot be significantised [*se significantiser*], which I call here the unnameable, can be pegged with a proper name. But the proper name does not come here as an index.

In 1975, it's different. Lacan posed the thesis according to which naming makes a hole, produces a holed real. He proposes as an example of a formula for the hole, which he borrows from the Bible: "I am that I am" – that's what a hole is, he says. A saying that makes a hole. Indeed, this phrase, from the fact of being emitted, supposes existence, but it is an utterance of ex-sistence, without its truth. It says neither jouissance, nor desire, nor even the name of the being that is called supreme – it only presentifies it by its saying. The translation of this phrase is contested, but that is not the problem here. The remark makes it possible to understand why Lacan says that what comes out of the hole are Names-of-the-Father, and not simply names or proper names. What comes out of the hole is saying, saying without saids, saying that itself makes a hole, father-God-saying [*dieure-père*]. The father here is reduced to making a hole, a hole that is necessary for the Borromean chain. There is no saying "que non" – to what would it say "que non" if in the hole of the unnameable there are no saids? The hole makes a saying [*fait dire*], makes a God-saying [*fait dieu-re*], the ex-sistent par excellence, as first condition of all of the names. All of the names, common names as well as unheard-of names, newly created names such as Cantor's aleph, or Lacan's R, S, I, come out of the hole and are produced from the saying of naming, from the God-saying that comes out of the hole. Essentially, the Names-of-the-Father are names of the hole. It is necessary to distinguish here the father as name, called Name-of-the-Father, and the father as naming [*nommant*]. Lacan says so explicitly in the lesson of April 15th: for each of us the knot is already made, "one is made from this act, x, by which the knot is made". Act and x! The naming as act [*nomination acte*], the fourth consistency, does not arise from the symbolic.

Here, we are not in the problematic of the proper name. We are far, you will agree, from daddy, mommy, and from the patronym that they transmitted according, moreover, to fluctuating legislations, and from the first name that they chose according to their fantasies of the moment. And yet we know the importance in the subjectivities of these two ways of transmitting the proper name, the relationship to the name inheriting the relationship to the Other, the traumatic parent. However, each speaking-being [*parlêtre*] has two proper names: the one from genealogy which is transmitted to him, which is received, and the one that he does not receive, which defines him in his singularity, his true proper name then, his symptom name, which is the name of his identity of desire and of jouissance. This is why, starting with "The subversion of the subject and the dialectic of desire", Lacan connected the proper name and S(A), written in the place of jouissance. When he says that the neurotic "is nameless [*un sans nom*]", this designates his relationship to his own symptom, a relationship that is at once a relationship of misrecognition [*méconnaissance*] and of rejection. We know how sensitive subjects are to the way they are seen, perceived, to the way others think of them, to what others could say about them, in a word, according to the most frequent formula, to what people reflect back to them [*à ce qu'on leur renvoie*]. Others reflect back to me that I am this and that, like this, like that, as if they were expecting not so much an interpretation as a verdict from the *vox populi*, the semblables, about what they are. This is what I named the mirror of the Other but it does not concern the image, it concerns being, the unnameable being who looks for a name. On the other hand, identifying with one's symptom marks the separation from the other, and if this happens in the end, it consists in assuming one's being of jouissance, even if enigmatic, namely in consenting to one's own name, the one that the subject had, but which he didn't want and didn't even know. His name can thus come to him through the saying of analysis.

Chapter XII

4th June 2014

I will close out the year with Lacan's final development regarding the father: the father is father of the name. From Oedipus to *Totem and Taboo* and *Moses and Monotheism*, Freud thought of the father as the condition, not only of humanisation, which I have been questioning this year, but also of what we call civilisation. Lacan, I have said, constantly oscillated between a virulent critique of the oedipal father and his reiterated approval of what would be the profound intuition of Freud. Hence the question: ultimately, what is his final word?

Freud was consumed with the question "what is a father?" This is certain. And indeed, father is a name, and we can ask regarding him: of what is father the name? The question does not bear only on a signified but on a referent, granted that – I believe I have insisted on this – what cannot be symbolised, what is then a remainder of the real in the symbolic, or despite the symbolic, can however be named, the act of naming [*nommer*] and the act of symbolising being two different things, and the first always has to do with a real.

Name and naming

This is what the thesis that I developed last time means, the thesis that says that the Names-of-the-Father, if they come out of the hole, the hole of the symbolic, as Lacan affirms, name the hole of the symbolic. The thesis is considered by many as being abstract, but the connection with Freud's formulas is easy. What Freud calls primal repression (PR) is a repression from which there is no return. We know his definition of repression: what is repressed are signifiers, and these repressed signifiers make their return in the formations of the unconscious and in free association. If there is no return, it is not excessive to recognise in primal repression a hole in the set of possible mobilisable signifiers. However, Freudian repression is not a simple absence of the signifier since, for him, the substance of the repressed is the drives. This hole that is void of signifiers is thus an animated hole, and is not inert: Lacan says it spits out names, Names-of-the-Father, names of the hole, I said. It's rather the names of what is lodged in the hole of the Symbolic and which does not pass through the signifier, whether we name it "the Thing" – as in the seminar *The Ethics of Psychoanalysis* – or jouissance – as in "The subversion of the subject and the dialectic of desire". In any case, concerning this hole that Freud named primal repression, Lacan also said that it is God in person; God is primal repression made person, the primal repression that would say – say for example, "I am that I am". Would this then be names of the very principle ... of animation?

There is thus a distinction between the function of the name, the fact of having or not having a name, and naming as act, between the Names-of-the-Father, the names of what we say is a father, and the naming father [*père nommant*], another father if I may say so, that Lacan introduces in *R.S.I.* You see, I suppose, that the distinction produced in "L'étourdit" between the saying and the saids is taken up here in the distinction between the saying of naming and the names that we give.

The Names-of-the-Father, names of the hole of the symbolic. This is so true that Lacan questions the holes of the rings of the imaginary and the real since in the knot, they also are holed. A distinction must be made between the hole of the symbolic – which takes after the structure of language, and which Lacan also wrote as S(A̸) – and the hole produced in the real, and moreover in the imaginary, by the hollowing out effect that the symbolic generates. One more remark about the real. Real is a word, but regarding this word, we can ask, "Of what it is the name?" If it is the name of what is outside the symbolic and outside the imaginary, we can say absolutely nothing more about it. In the first pages of *Le Sinthome*, it is this impossibility that Lacan evokes when speaking of nature and which he defines as that which is excluded from what we name. And, indeed, what of it we name attaches itself to the field of language. And so, the real about which we speak is always, in some ways, relative to what is named, and as a result it is knotted to other consistencies. All of the expressions that we employ about the real include it: the real in the symbolic or of the symbolic, this is the impossible; the real holed by the symbolic, this is another real, the real of what is living [*du vivant*], the real outside the imaginary, the real expelled from meaning, always a remainder then, etc. Hence Lacan's expression "the real is not One". There are thus reals for the one who speaks and, at the beginning of *Le Sinthome*, he says: "nature is not One". I have said it before, but I must insist on it.

So, three holes and Lacan goes on to say that the holes of the imaginary and the real must also be in some ways producers of names. I quote: "It is not only the symbolic that has the privilege of Names-of-the-Father." More precisely, in the lesson of March 11th we find: "The Names-of-the-Father, this is what it is – the symbolic, the imaginary, the real. These are the primary names [*noms premiers*] insofar as they name something." On March 18th, he insists that if imaginary, symbolic, and real are Names-of-the-Father, it is because "it is in these names that the knot holds". Without them then, there is no Borromean knot. This remark implies very well what I have already pointed out: if the name can be called father, Name-of-the-Father, it is on account of its power to generate – here, the knot. On the other hand, he also poses that "for the knot, naming is a fourth element." Naming is not a Name-of-the-Father, it is the condition of it. The Names-of-the-Father give names to the holes, all three of them; however, naming in act is a fourth element. And Lacan goes on to distinguish in addition to these three names, the three namings that give them names. He gives a schema for the imaginary and symbolic naming, but for the real naming, he slows down and he questions. Having specified that giving a name is certainly a symbolic naming, but limited to the symbolic, he asks himself: "The father, is he the one who gave things their name, or should he be examined at the level of the real. Is it not necessary to tie the term of naming to the level of the circle from which we support the real?" Just before, he had called to mind the distinction between giving a name and the creationist idea of *fiat lux* – the true power of the saying that, more than naming what is, engenders it.

And then, surprise, he refers the three namings to three names of the affects of the one who speaks, three names already produced by Freud. "Naming of the imaginary as inhibition, naming of the real as anxiety, naming of the symbolic, the blossom of the symbolic itself, as symptom." How should we hear this? Lacan didn't explain himself any more than this because the following year, he moved on to Joyce. What is certain is that with these three words, *inhibition, symptom, anxiety*, Freud gave a name to three clinical phenomena experienced by those who speak, three names that designate, in advance, these three other Names-of-the-Father that are Imaginary, Symbolic, and Real, which were produced by Lacan. This is the most obvious reading. We can hear it in this way, unless we suppose that these three clinical phenomena themselves function as a fourth naming term, as placeholder then of a saying of naming of the holes of the imaginary, the symbolic, and the real. This is something to be explored.

I am insisting on these extremely complex developments because Lacan looks, and not without difficulty, to overturn the whole of his earlier doctrine, linguistics and logic, in the schema of the Borromean knot, this knot from which he expected some new perspective on the analytic clinic. And probably he did not have the time to bring it to fruition and to resolve the contradictions that we can identify in the final seminars. An example: on March 11th, he says, "name giving" is part of the symbolic, and on May 13th, "the entire question is one of knowing if naming arises, as it seems, apparently, from the symbolic. [...] For my knot, naming is a fourth element" – which is then not a part of the symbolic. It is on account of these fumblings that I pose the question of knowing what remains certain concerning the function of the Borromean knot, and in parallel with the reformulations of the father-function.

A new father

There is nothing questionable about what Lacan pursues: namely, bringing out a "father" function, disjoined from all significations that are attached to this term in the tradition that Freud did not subvert. Translated into Lacan's terms, the question is precisely that of creative significance, the engendering significance of naming in act – I insist, an existential naming – itself named *sinthome*, the fourth element, distinct from the three consistencies, but as the condition of their knotting. The father, the name father [*nom de père*], connotes in *lalangue*, in any case, a power of "generation", of engendering, which can be distinguished from what specifies the mother. The mother, as such, is the term that designates the reproductive power of bodies. It is not done without a genitor, certainly, in any case without a spermatozoon, but the father as such is not the generating function. It is another engendering that is designated by the term father, even if the primary signification is that of the genitor. This is why, moreover, even if parthenogenesis were to succeed and render the genitor superfluous, the question of the father would not be resolved for all that. Lacan insisted on this from the beginning and the entire Freudian development supposes it. In 1975, he takes up in terms of Borromean knotting what he formulated over the course of the years concerning the father-function with its clinical significance, the function of naming being the condition of the Borromean knot.

I said last time that with this we are far from daddy, mommy, and the surname that they transmitted, but let me add: we are far only if we do not want, or if we cannot grasp that the clinic is structured. Those who like the concrete, as we say, will read with interest what Lacan specifies about this hole, and which indicates the clinical significance of it, when he says first of all that "the interdiction of incest is the hole of the symbolic", and also that the knot is what knots the couple despite the sexual relationship that does not exist, and also that the social knot stands in [*supplée*] for the relationship that is lacking, and so on. Here we are once again on familiar territory: incest, the hetero couple, the social link, and it would be necessary to add more generally, love. Let me now turn to this.

What makes incest the hole of the symbolic? In tradition, or rather traditions, that of the Hindus for example (which Lacan evokes), sleeping with one's mother is forbidden ... by the father. But this interdiction of the Other – in the double sense of *of*, an interdiction from the Other and which bears on the Other – this transgression [*faute*] that is represented by images of sleeping with the mother, mythifies in fact an impossible that derives from the structure of language, which is not historical but structural. The fact that Freud evoked the jouissance of all of the women in order to designate a jouissance that would be absolute, which would not fall under the sway of the negativity of language, indicates it because all of the women is clearly an impossible. There is no need for myth, however. All that is necessary is language and what it implies of the castration of jouissance, in fact. All that is necessary is real effects of the signifier, which are not effects of symbolisation, but rather of negativisation and of the parcelling out of jouissance. This begins with the minimal symbolisation of *Fort/Da* because from this moment on, the mother is lost. The interdiction of incest, Lacan says, "is propagated on the side of castration". Indeed, why does tradition convoke the father? To give an account of the limitation of jouissance, that is, of the hole in jouissance. What Lacan shows is that the hole is the impossible of the jouissance of the Other owing to the structure of language. From this hole, came the father as name, the interdicting father, in order to think the impossible experienced in the so-called sexual act, the impossible of the access to the Other that seemed unthinkable. The father as name personifies the principle of limitation. But Lacan points out that this myth does not suffice for understanding the link between castration and the interdiction of incest.

The link, he says, is my sexual non-relationship. Indeed, it is important to understand that the interdiction does not imply the inevitability of castration. On the contrary, it leaves room for thinking that transgression would make access to the jouissance of the Other possible. It thus allows the mirage of the sexual relationship to subsist. But castration does not arise from an interdiction that has come from the symbolic – it is a real.

Let me turn now to sex. It falls under the sway of the function of the name, of the receiving of a name. To name [*nommer*] is to introduce some "distinctivity" into the real. Something is only distinguished because it is named, Lacan says at the beginning of *Le Sinthome*. For sex, there is only a boy-girl difference because it is named. Even if we rectify the grammatical genders of pronouns as we have started to do, this difference, because it is named, will last all the same, so long as we don't get rid of the mention of masculine and feminine sex on identity cards and on official documents. This is already the case in certain countries for individuals whose anatomy at birth is ambiguous. This is the case of those who contest the name that has been attributed to them, transsexuals, but for the rest, the others who are more numerous, even the theories of gender haven't gotten to the point of putting into question these names that are given to them: man and woman. How do we get from the named difference – which relies on anatomy and, beyond it, on the real heterogeneity of jouissances, which have always been known – to the couple? Not without the Borromean knot, Lacan answers at this time. If we depict the two sexes, let us say the two names of jouissance, with two unknotted circles because of the non-relationship, it is necessary to have a third that knots them to make a couple, although there is no relationship. That they be knotted, from the fact of being unknotted, signals the necessity of the recourse to the Borromean knot. Since the dawn of time, Lacan notes, we have spoken of the knots of love in order to designate what attaches, hitches these two distinct unities. Notice that before this Borromean formalisation, the function of the phallus was already implicitly nodal for the sexed couple – the phallus being at once the signifier of the difference of bodies, and the connecting signifier of the two sexes since man and woman have a relationship here and identify through it, with a being and with a having. Hence, the reference where Lacan identifies the phallus with the infinite line constitutive of the knot. There is no couple that holds that is not Borromean. As for the social knot that stands in [*supplée*] for the sexual non-relationship, it also passes through the name, the giving name of naming implying the social link. I have developed this point in detail elsewhere.

Not without the father

To name [*nommer*], which you could write *n'hommer*, Lacan says in the lesson of March 18th, writing with the *h* of *homme* [man] – *n'hommer* is an act. Suffice it to say that naming [*nomination*] makes the man. It does so because the *naming*[1] makes the knot of the semblant and the real. It is naming that became the humanising function. In "The subversion of the subject and the dialectic of desire", Lacan affirmed that the father is the one who unites a desire to the law; the law being that of the interdiction of incest, which is in fact the law of the symbolic as holed. In 1975, with this naming as fourth element, the father of the name is father of the knot.

The trajectory is clear. What is posed in linguistic terms with the problematic of the signifying chain, S(Ⱥ), and then with the inaccessible two of the "no such thing as a sexual relationship", is represented in the knot by the hole of the symbolic, the symbolic as holed. But the impasse of language, S(Ⱥ) has repercussions at the level of the real, at the level of sexed bodies, and what's more, it governs bodies, programming castration, making a law of the "*Y a d'l'Un*" and of the inaccessible two of the sexual relationship. From here on out, humanisation, namely the possibility of a link, whether this is the link of the couple, "of each man [*chacun*] to each woman [*chacune*]", or the social link, becomes a problem. How are "unarities", these "proletarian" individuals – who have nothing to make a social link, as Lacan says in "La troisième" – linked? Lacan responded to this first of all with the construction of the discourses, these discourses that do not include all who speak – there are some who are outside discourse. And by the formulas of sexuation which do not guarantee an order between the sexes, but which try to explain the distribution of jouissances once there is only a semblant of sex, the phallus, and no sexual discourse. Then, by the Borromean knot, as condition, not only of the "real subject", but as the condition of links, at once of the link of the couple and of the social link, which suppose the knotting of the real and the semblant, but also for the subjects of the link of desire and jouissance. There is no way of conceiving a desire, Lacan says, without the Borromean knot. Indeed, the object *a* lodges itself at the wedging point [*point de coincement*] of the three consistencies, thus holing the imaginary and the real as much as the symbolic.

I conclude: Lacan recused Freud's Oedipus complex, but not the father as principle of humanisation. He even tried to demonstrate the necessity of it, first as a necessity of the logical exception, then as a naming function, the necessary condition of the Borromean knot. It is the culmen of what Lacan elaborated concerning the generating function of the father, generator of the knot of the three consistencies for each individual and of the possible links between individuals. Shall we then say: no socialisation without the father? Yes, except that this father that is necessary as an ex-sistential naming function is not necessarily a father, and does not imply sex. I have already developed this.[2] To say it with some emphasis, the father of the name does without the father of the oedipal metaphor. This is quite necessary if we want to take seriously the affirmation according to which analytic discourse does without the father.

But fatherless

Lacan affirmed this over and over. In "Radiophonie", speaking of analytic discourse, such as he writes it, in which the object *a* is at the place of the semblant, he specifies the "without recourse to the Name-of-the-Father" of this discourse. *Le sinthome* evokes a "doing without the father", a famous formula, this name "to be lost in perpetuity". It is strange this "in perpetuity", which cannot fail to evoke perpetuation, the perpetuation of generations, which we attribute to the father in the common sense. It would thus be necessary to lose it as long as we attribute this perpetuation to him. Obviously, if we do without the name, the name to be lost [*nom à perdre*], keeping only the function, as I say Lacan did, the name father is no longer there, or should no longer be there. All that remains is the function, but Lacan still names it Father by saying the father of the name. This lends itself to all of the misunderstandings, by which I mean all of the surreptitious returns of the cute little oedipal story [*historiole*] that today's Lacanians are far from avoiding. It is justified, however, from the fact that naming has the power of engendering. It is indeed necessary that this function be present in the saying of psychoanalysis for Lacan to be able to affirm, without contradiction, that we both do without the father and that we make use of him. "Doing without the father, on the condition of making use of him", or, another formula, psychoanalysis makes itself "the dupe of the father" (Lacan, 1979, p. 36). Doing without the name of the father, then, and making use of the function, whether we define it by the "*dire que non* [saying that no]" – it is not what is said that is to be interpreted – or rather ultimately by the "*dire qui noue* [the saying that knots]". Indeed, chit chat does not only produce meaning. Through the "*naming*",[3] the *nomination* [naming] that is not communication, through "the naming [*le nommer*], the giving name, the consecrating of a thing with a speaking name, [...] chit chat knots itself to something real" (Lacan, 1974–1975, lesson of March 11th 1975). In other words, chit chat in analysis is what Lacan calls an "operational reality [*réalité opératoire*]" because its saying has real effects. Lacan specified this operation: in order to obtain a meaning, we make a splice between the imaginary and the symbolic, that is to say, unconscious knowledge, but "we make of it, in one blow, another, between what is symbolic and what is real, between the *sinthome* and the real, parasite of jouissance" (Lacan, 2005, p. 73). In other words, in operating with meaning, we also operate with the knot. Analytic speech – where the saying of demand and the saying of interpretation criss-cross – this analytic speech, as "operational reality", knots. To make use of the function without the name is to make use of the knotting function, the *sinthome* – the *sinthome* being another name of the knotting function.

I showed with the example of Joyce, and in contradiction with what is usually said about it, that the restoration of the knot goes through meaning. The "lapsus of the Borromean knot" in Joyce is the fact that the imaginary is not knotted. According to Lacan, the episode of the beating that he receives from his buddies, which produces no affect of retribution in him, which indicates that he does not identify with his body, is evidence of this. Another evidence of this – I have already developed this – is this unreadable writing of *Finnegans Wake*, which handles the play of letters without an aim of meaning. A writing then that knots directly the symbolic of language, of languages, and the real of jouissance. The well-known thesis formulated by Lacan is that Joyce corrected this flaw of the knot with his ego name. But it was not enough to declare as artist this ego name. The actual operation goes through his art, Borromean art, Lacan says, which supposes meaning. As a result, Joyce joined the imaginary to the knot of the symbolic and the real, which specifies his writing through this production of meaning, and even a unique meaning, which is ... the enigma. It is through the enigma that his art is Borromean. It is his enigmatic enunciation that allows Lacan to say that his art is Borromean, whereas his writing in *Finnegans Wake* is not. The enunciation, "is the enigma carried over into the power of writing", Lacan says. It's true. Even in analysis, where interpretation should not name "what is said"[4] but the "that one says", because it is the cause of the saying, of the saying that no word represents, which leaves a writing trace within the discourse where it is produced. Similarly, he who in *Stephen Hero* said that he wanted to decipher "the enigma of his position in his own way" (Joyce, 1977, p. 186), makes himself represented by this calculated enigma that is *Finnegans Wake*. At the time of *Finnegans Wake*, the work with which Joyce most identified, he gave up resolving this enigma, and instead, he makes himself to be represented by it. He identifies with it in some ways, and he signs with what I now call his "enigma name", a name by which he supports the *ego* that corrects the unknotting of the imaginary. It is this same power of the act of enunciation, of the generating saying, that is at work in analysis, this time in the oral register and not in the scriptural. It's not nothing to observe that with this enigma name, Joyce also re-established a social link, with everything that that implies of libidinal circulation.

Suffice to say that the father-function can be fatherless. It is fatherless in every case where a *suppléance* staves off psychosis, but above all it is fatherless in analytic discourse, and we can from then on conclude that the knotting function is contingent, possibly ceases "to not be written" – this is the definition of the contingent – without a father being at fault. This is even what is implied by the idea that a father is a symptom, namely a configuration, amongst other things, of the knots of the semblant and of the real of jouissance. We see what gives rise to this fatherless father-function, which can be lacking without a father being lacking, foreclosure, but which can also be borne by a father who "deserves respect", a symptom, but who can above all be stood in [*supplée*] for and born without a father, by other symptoms. With this, Lacan managed to complete the disconnection of this function from the structures of the family and society, and in particular from the programs of what we call tradition. These are themes that I have already highlighted in *Lacan: The Unconscious Reinvented* (2014). The saying that names is an event, outside the program, outside anticipation, and thus opens onto the field of possibles, of "what ceases to be written" of the solitude of proletarian bodies, that is to say, outside the social link.

In closing, Lacan's trajectory seems clear to me. After this big flash [*éclat*], in the double sense of the term, that was "The function and field of speech and of language" with its promotion of the symbolic, of the famous full speech that made a link and supposed the button-tying father of all of discourse, he highlighted what constitutes *his* hypothesis, namely that language has real effects, on the real of what is living [*du vivant*], the subtraction of *a* which causes desire and parcels out jouissance (hence the formulas at the beginning of *Le Sinthome*, the S_2 splits between the symbol and the symptom). These effects have nothing humanising about them. On the contrary, they are disharmonious, and what's more, dissociating. The unconscious, as much as it is confused with the symbolic, has dissociating effects. I developed this at the beginning of the year. Even the desire that goes towards the other body has a destructive impact. It "a-nnuls" the other. From this, the problem of humanisation became crucial for Lacan. I have already cited this phrase that says that oedipal ideology and "the specific attachment of the analyst to the coordinates of the family, […] is linked to a mode of questioning sexuality that seriously risks missing a sexual conversion that is taking place before our eyes" (Lacan, 2001d, p. 587). What is it? The end of the regency of the norms of hetero-sexuality, and the newfound freedom [*nouveau droit de cité*] of so-called perverse jouissances that are all situated with respect to the object *a*. It is not by chance if it is at the end of *Anxiety*, after having constructed the object *a*, that Lacan introduces the function of the name as that which reduces anxiety – that he next highlights the "not anonymous" desire, the one that is pegged with a name, and which transmits a name. I could say a name with Borromean effects.

The question remaining is one of knowing if the father of the name introduced in *R.S.I.* is Lacan's final development on this subject and if what he then pursued with the Borromean knots changes something here. This is what I did not explore this year. I think, however, that the function of the name was always more prevalent after *R.S.I.* I give as proof what he introduces as a fatherless naming for Joyce in this seminar, and what he takes up in his conference "Joyce le symptôme II", which comes after it, I think. He says: I name Joyce with the name that is his. We find here the distinction of the Name, and even of the proper name, and of naming which, in this precise case, names the name that is already there. With this additional indication, that the name is the symptom name. This is the true proper name that pegs unique singularity. This symptom name is a name of separation, that is not received from the other, a secret name in some ways. But in naming one who speaks with his own symptom name, the act of naming connects him to a social link; in the present case, by the grace of Lacan, Joyce is connected to that of psychoanalysis. It is another name and another link than that which he made for himself with his artist name of the enigma. In psychoanalysis, identifying with one's symptom, if that happens at the end, is to assume one's being of jouissance, even if opaque, that is, to consent to one's own name, the one that the subject had but which he didn't want and which he didn't even know. His symptom name can thus come to him through analysis and sometimes even be re-named by the saying of analysis. This is obviously what is at stake in the pass.

Notes

1 [In English in the original]
2 See: Soler, C. (2014). *Lacan: The Unconscious Reinvented*. E. Faye and S. Schwartz (Trans.). London: Karnac.
3 [In English in the original].
4 See the "Postface au *Seminar XI*" (Lacan, 2001b).

References

Joyce, J. (1977). *Stephen Hero: Part of the First Draft of a Portrait of the Artist as a Young Man*. T. Spencer (Ed.). Frogmore: Triad/Panther Books.
Lacan, J. (1967). Discours de clôture des journées sur les psychoses. *Recherches* n° 8.
Lacan, J. (1968). La méprise du sujet supposé savoir. *Scilicet* n° 1. Paris: Éditions du Seuil (also in *Autres écrits*. Paris: Éditions du Seuil).
Lacan, J. (1970). Radiophonie. *Scilicet* n° 2/3. Paris: Éditions du Seuil (also in: *Autres écrits*. Paris: Éditions du Seuil, 2001).
Lacan, J. (1973). L'étourdit. *Scilicet* n° 4. Paris: Éditions du Seuil (also in: *Autres écrits*. Paris: Éditions du Seuil, 2001).
Lacan, J. (1974–1975). *R.S.I.* (Unpublished manuscript).
Lacan, J. (1974). *Télévision*. Paris: Éditions du Seuil.
Lacan, J. (1975a). ... ou pire. Compte rendu du Séminaire 1971–1972. *Scilicet* n° 5. Paris: Éditions du Seuil (also in: *Autres écrits*. Paris: Éditions du Seuil).
Lacan, J. (1975b). Introduction à l'édition allemande d'un premier volume des *Écrits*. *Scilicet* n° 5. Paris: Éditions du Seuil (also in: *Autres écrits*. Paris: Éditions du Seuil, 2001).
Lacan, J. (1979). Joyce le symptôme II. In: J. Aubert (Ed.). *Joyce avec Lacan*. Paris: Navarin, 1987.
Lacan, J. (1984a). Compte rendu du Séminaire 1966–1967: La logique du fantasme. *Ornicar?* 29. Paris: Navarin (also in: *Autres écrits*. Paris, Éditions du Seuil, 2001).
Lacan, J. (1984b). Compte rendu du Séminaire 1967–1968: L'acte psychanalytique. *Ornicar?* 29. Paris: Navarin (also in: *Autres écrits*. Paris, Éditions du Seuil, 2001).
Lacan, J. (1984c [1938]). *Les complexes familiaux dans la formation de l'individu*. Paris: Navarin (also in: *Autres écrits*. Paris: Éditions du Seuil, 2001).
Lacan, J. (1985 [1975]). Conférence à Genève sur le symptôme. In: *Le Bloc-notes de la psychanalyse* n° 5.
Lacan, J. (1992). *The Seminar of Jacques Lacan, Book VII: The Ethics of Psychoanalysis (1959–1960)*. D. Porter (Trans.). New York: W. W. Norton.
Lacan, J. (1998a). *Le Séminaire de Jacques Lacan, Livre IV, La relation d'objet (1956–1957)*. Paris: Éditions du Seuil.
Lacan, J. (1998b). *Le Séminaire de Jacques Lacan, Livre V, Les formations de l'inconscient (1957–1958)*. Paris: Éditions du Seuil.
Lacan, J. (1998c [1977]). Preface to the English-Language Edition. In: *The Four Fundamental Concepts of Psychoanalysis, The Seminar of Jacques Lacan, Book XI*. A. Sheridan (Trans.). New York: W. W. Norton.

Lacan, J. (1998d). *The Four Fundamental Concepts of Psychoanalysis, The Seminar of Jacques Lacan, Book XI*. A. Sheridan (Trans.). New York: W. W. Norton.

Lacan, J. (1999). *The Seminar of Jacques Lacan, Book XX, Encore: On feminine sexuality, the limits of love and knowledge (1972–1973)*. B. Fink (Trans.). New York: W. W. Norton.

Lacan, J. (2001a [1970]). Préface à une thèse. In: *Autres écrits*. Paris: Éditions du Seuil.

Lacan, J. (2001b [1973]). Postface au *Seminar XI*. In: *Autres écrits*. Paris: Éditions du Seuil.

Lacan, J. (2001c [1976]). Préface à l'édition anglaise du *Séminaire XI*. In: *Autres écrits*. Paris: Éditions du Seuil.

Lacan, J. (2001d [1978]). Première version de la "Proposition du 9 Octobre 1967 sur le psychanalyste de l'École." In: *Autres écrits*. Paris: Éditions du Seuil.

Lacan, J. (2005). *Le Séminaire de Jacques Lacan, Livre XXIII, Le Sinthome (1975–1976)*. Paris: Éditions du Seuil.

Lacan, J. (2006 [1946]). Presentation on psychical causality. In: *Écrits: The First Complete Edition in English*. B. Fink (Trans.). New York: W. W. Norton.

Lacan, J. (2006 [1957–1958]). On a question prior to any possible treatment of psychosis. In: *Écrits: The First Complete Edition in English*. B. Fink (Trans.). New York: W. W. Norton.

Lacan, J. (2006 [1958a]). The direction of the treatment and the principles of its power. In: *Écrits: The First Complete Edition in English*. B. Fink (Trans.). New York: W. W. Norton.

Lacan, J. (2006 [1958b]). The signification of the phallus [Die Bedeutung des Phallus]. In: *Écrits: The First Complete Edition in English*. B. Fink (Trans.). New York: W. W. Norton.

Lacan, J. (2006 [1960a]). Remarks on Daniel Lagache's presentation: "Psychoanalysis and personality structure". In: *Écrits: The First Complete Edition in English*. B. Fink (Trans.). New York: W. W. Norton.

Lacan, J. (2006 [1960b]). Subversion of the subject and the dialectic of desire in the Freudian unconscious. In: *Écrits: The First Complete Edition in English*. B. Fink (Trans.). New York: W. W. Norton.

Lacan, J. (2006 [1963]). Kant with Sade. In: *Écrits: The First Complete Edition in English*. B. Fink (Trans). New York: W. W. Norton.

Lacan, J. (2006 [1964]). Position of the unconscious. In: *Écrits: The First Complete Edition in English*. B. Fink (Trans.). New York: W. W. Norton.

Lacan, J. (2006 [1966]). Science and truth. In: *Écrits: The First Complete Edition in English*. B. Fink (Trans.). New York: W. W. Norton.

Lacan, J. (2015). *The Seminar of Jacques Lacan, Book VIII: Transference* (1960–1961). B. Fink (Trans.). Cambridge: Polity.

Lacan, J. (2016). *The Seminar of Jacques Lacan, Book X: Anxiety*. A. R. Price (Trans.). Cambridge: Polity.

Soler, C. (2014). *Lacan: The Unconscious Reinvented*. E. Faye and S. Schwartz (Trans.). London: Karnac.

Index

Adam's rib myth, 13, 38
Alcibiades, 28
alienation, 48
analysand, 12, 16, 36–9, 45, 59, 60; as agent, 61–2
analyst, 80; desire of, 23–4, 31–3, 36–40; fall, representation of, 45; naming and, 90
analytic act, 37–42, 83, 90
analytic discourse, 41, 44, 49, 60, 61–3, 70
Antigone, 3, 23, 27–9
anxiety, 2, 20, 28, 32, 96
Aristotle, 58, 77, 80

Badiou, Alain, 54
being: naming and, 89, 91, 99; question of, 12–13
"The beyond of the Oedipus complex" (Soler), 63
biological heritage, 79, 84
body, 1; desire and, 24; jouissance and, 10–11; language effects on, 7; named difference, 99; Other and, 14; subject speaks with, 15
Borromean knot, 17, 22, 35, 41, 54, 88; hole of the symbolic, 53, 92, 93, 96; introduction of, 10, 12; naming and, 98–101; unarity, 36, 39–40
Borromean subject, 39–40

capitalism, ix, 2, 5, 8, 64; body and, 22–3; not-all of society, 84–5
Cassin, Barbara, 45
castration, 4, 8, 13, 46, 54, 58; discourse and, 62–3, 79; father dissociated from, 58; father of law of, 50; function of, 67–8, 71; incest interdiction and, 98–9; lack of, 24; not-all of women and, 83–4; as real, 99

child, 1, 10–11; generalised, 5–6; symptom and, 15–16
civilisation, 16, 44–5, 95
coastline metaphor, 74, 78, 82–3
colonisation, ix, 1–2
comedy of the sexes, 67
comprehension, 59, 60n3
Critique of Pure Reason (Kant), 61

death, 3, 12, 73
de Las Casas, Bartolomé, 2
denatured, the, 10–11
deposition [*destitution*], 28, 31, 38
desire, 3, 8; of analyst, 23–4, 31–3, 36–40; destructivity of, 26, 27–9, 30–2, 35, 38; dialectic of, 34, 36, 99–100; of father, 25–6, 30; as fixed, 15, 22–3, 31, 34; graph of, 30, 47, 54, 60, 61, 93; humanisation of, viii, 31, 34–5; idealisation of, 23–4, 26, 28, 31–2, 40; *l'(a)cause première*, 29–30, 34–5; lack and loss, 12–13, 24, 29–30, 33, 65; of mother (DM), 49, 51, 53–4; paradoxes of, 8, 23, 32–3, 39; phallic signification of, 49, 65–7; as satisfaction, 32, 68; tragedy of, 27–9, 30; types of desires, 32–6; value of, 23–4, 28–9; want-to-be, 12, 13, 24, 30
destiny, 27–8
Deutsch, Helene, 88
discourse, 40–2; outside, 54, 62; psychosis as outside, 54, 78, 80; saying as exception, 58–60; suppléance and, 62–3, 78–9, 82; women excluded from, 84. *See also* language
dit-mension, 78, 85n2
domination, relationship of, 49–50
drawers of thought, 80–1

drives, 3, 4, 8, 10, 42, 48; as effects of language, 34; genesis of, 14–18; partial, 21; signifiers of, 30

ego, 28, 42, 101
Elementary Structures of Kinship (Lévi-Strauss), 3
Emile (Rousseau), 10–11
enunciation, 59, 102
etiquette (*éthiquette*), 40
exception: function of, 56–8, 65–8; saying as, 58–60, 74; universal and, 73, 77–8
existentialism, 3
ex-sistence, 7, 17, 58–60, 74–6, 77; father of the name and, 88; God-saying [*dieu-re*], 87, 93

family: bourgeois, conjugal, 21, 45, 49, 76; domination, 49–50; hyper-modernity and, 85
father: but fatherless, 100–3; classical, 76; dead, 75; desire of, 25–6, 30; *dit que non* [says that no], 87, 88; exception, function of, 56–8; exception, saying as, 58–60; heterosexuality in relation to, 47–8, 62; of the name, 87, 88–9; name of the Thing, 51–2; naming and, 46, 96; new function, 96–8; not without, 99–100; paternal order, 48–51; perorating utang [*pérorant outang*], 46, 56, 65, 74; as person, 75–6; phallic function and, 69–72; phallus without, 25–6, 69–70, 99–100; as saying, 73, 88–9; saying-father, 75; as signifier, 49–50, 75. *See also* Name-of-the-Father; paternal metaphor
Finnegans Wake (Joyce), 101–2
fixion, 15, 41
foreclosure, 57, 83–4, 88, 102
formation, 4, 8, 10, 20
for-not-alling [*pourpastouter*], 85
Fort/Da, 11–12, 13, 98
Foucault, Michel, 5
free association, 44–5
free will, 3
Frege, Gottlob, 55, 58, 67, 70, 73, 75
Freud, Sigmund, 1, 30, 42, 95, 96; castration complex, 21; *Fort/Da*, 11–12; free association, 44–5; saying and, 59–60; unconscious, 7; women, view of, 83; Works: *Beyond the Pleasure Principle*, 5; *Interpretation of Dreams*, 12; *Introductory Lectures on Psychoanalysis*, 16; *Three Essays on the Theory of Sexuality*, 66, 68; *Totem and Taboo*, 56, 65, 74

function: of castration, 67–8, 71; of exception, 56–8; of father, in Oedipus complex, 44–8, 50, 52n1, 56; of father, new, 96–8; of name, 89–91; of naming, 91–4; normative, 47–8. *See also* parental function
function, 65–8; of phallus, 69–73; phallus before father, 70; propositional, 73–4; speech as cause, 69–72

Gaucher, Maurice, 6
genealogy, 90, 93
generations, 27–8, 44, 100–1
genitalisation, 47
genital oblativity, 31
genital phase, 42
genitor, father function and, 74, 76, 88, 98, 100
Ginés de Sepúlveda, Juan, 2
God, 33, 35, 96
Gödel, Kurt, 57, 73
Godelier, Maurice, 44
God-saying [*dieu-re*], 87–8, 89, 93
Gorki, Maxim, 1
grammar, 61, 73

half-saying, 87–8, 92
Hamlet, 23
hedonism, 3–4
hetero-sexuality, 16, 21, 31, 64–5, 103; phallic signification and, 65–7; in relation to father, 47–8, 62; two halves of couple, 42, 62–3, 66, 77–80, 88
hole: of Other, 5, 12, 58, 92–3, 95; of symbolic, 5, 12, 53, 92–3, 95–8
homosexuality, 16, 21, 31, 42, 103
humanisation, viii–ix, 1–4, 10, 95; denaturing, 10–11; of desire, viii, 31, 34–5; father, function of, 44; of natural being, 10–11
humanitarianery, ix, 1–2
hyper-modernity, 85
hysteria, 32, 33, 61–2, 87

idealisation, 23–4, 26, 28, 31–2
identification, 87, 93, 103; sexed, 42, 66
imaginary, 20, 22, 69; of body, 70; comedy of the sexes, 67; hole of, 96–7; metaphor and, 48–9; naming and, 91
impossible, the, 41
incest, 98–9, 99–100
inhibition, 96
inhuman, 2, 7–8
instinct, 19–20

interpretation, 60
intimacy, 64

Jones, Ernest, 32
joui-sens, 22
jouissance, viii, 3–4, 7, 8, 8–9n3; body and, 10–11; castrated, 8, 67–8, 71, 77, 98; feminine, 41; fitted out, 19–26; "hetero," 16, 21; limitation on, 4, 10–11, 15, 26, 34, 42–3, 56, 70, 98; phallic and penile, 16–17, 20–2, 70; of phallus, 67–8, 69–72, 78–9; in place of the Other, 82; speech and, 69–72; surplus, 2, 33, 38, 44–5; as symptom, 34; want-to-enjoy, 13
Joyce, James, 90, 96, 101–2

Kant, Immanuel, 35–6, 61
knowledge, 16, 19–20; desire for, 39; horror of, 27, 31; RUCS and, 7, 71

Lacan, Jacques, viii–ix, 1; on colonisation, ix, 1–2; conformism and, 47–8; logions of, 45; unsigned works, 91; *Works and Seminars:* "Analytic act," 37; *Anxiety,* 8, 13, 24, 25, 30, 58, 68, 103; *Les complexes familiaux,* 45; "Compte rendu de l'acte analytique," 19, 38, 40; "D'écolage," 42; *Desire and its Interpretation,* 23, 24, 26; "Direction of the treatment," 23, 24, 29; *D'un discours qui ne serait pas du semblant,* 62, 70–2, 75; *Écrits,* 4, 19, 24, 40, 50, 57; *Encore,* 7, 11–12, 14, 16, 20, 31, 41, 53, 55, 60, 68, 71; *Ethics of Psychoanalysis,* 3, 23, 26, 27–9, 53, 55, 68, 92, 95; "L'étourdit," 31, 40–2, 46, 55, 58–60, 61–6, 69–70, 72–5, 77–82, 84–5, 87–8, 96; *Les formations de l'inconscient,* 47, 50, 56; *Four Fundamental Concepts of Psychoanalysis,* 13, 16, 22, 30, 34, 46; "The function and field of speech and language," 15, 20; Geneva conference, 70; "The instance of the letter in the unconscious," 6, 15, 18, 22, 36; "L'introduction à l'édition allemande des *Écrits,*" 72; *Kant with Sade,* 36, 61; *Lituraterre,* 78; *The Names-of-the-Father,* 46, 51, 54–6; "On a question prior to any possible treatment of psychosis," 12, 47, 50; "... ou pire" (*Scilicet 5*), 24–5, 46, 59–60, 64, 72; "Position of the unconscious," 13, 14, 25, 30, 48; "Preface to the English translation of Seminar XI," 7, 19, 24; "La proposition sur le psychanalyste de l'École"
(1967), 23–4, 39, 45; *The Psychoses,* 47; "Radiophonie," 8, 10, 14, 41, 55, 61–2, 64, 78, 100; *La relation d'objet,* 17, 47; "Remarks on Daniel Lagache's presentation," 14, 75; *R.S.I.,* 15, 17, 19, 20–1, 25–6, 35, 39–40, 65, 74–6, 87, 92, 96, 103; "Le savoir du psychanalyste," 5, 81; "Science and truth," 17; *Scilicet,* 24–5, 46, 59–60, 64, 72, 91; *Seminar I,* 26; *Seminar XI,* 14; "The signification of the phallus," 29; *Le Sinthome,* 19, 40, 45, 68, 69–70, 96, 100, 102; "The subversion of the subject and the dialectic of desire," 14, 57–8, 63–4, 69, 92–3, 95–6; "Le symptôme," 15; *Television,* 8, 55, 83, 89, 90; *Transference,* 26, 27, 39; "La troisième," 10, 100
Lacan, lecteur de Joyce (Soler), 72
Lacan: The Unconscious Reinvented (Soler), 6, 102
lack and loss, 29–30, 33, 65, 69, 82; vocabulary of, 12–13, 24, 29
La Controverse de Valladolid, 2
lalangue, 7, 10, 14, 16, 19, 29, 69, 71, 74, 76; naming and, 97. *See also* language
L and R schemas, 47, 57, 66, 66–7, 69
language, 2–5, 50–1, 78; as brake/limit, viii, 4, 10; chain of metaphor and metonymy, 8, 28–9; as dead, 14; desire as effect of, 27, 34; discourse, 40–2; *dit-mension,* 78, 85n2; effect of, 7–8; grammar, 61, 73; jouissance, fitted out with, 19–26; lack and loss, vocabulary of, 12–13, 24, 29; logic of, 40–3, 48, 73; name of the Thing, 53–4; negativising effect, 4, 32; paternal metaphor, 6–7; structure of, 7–8, 41, 54, 59–61, 96, 98; synchrony of, 47. *See also* discourse; lalangue
law, 35–6, 44, 50; desire and, 99–100; exception and, 56–7
lecton (λεκτὸν), 55
"L'étourdit" (Lacan), 31, 40–2, 46, 77–82; function of father, 55, 58–60, 61–6, 69–70, 72–5; naming, 87–8, 96; not-all society, 84–5
letter, 15, 17–18, 36, 53, 74; substitution, 20–1
Lévi-Strauss, Claude, 3
libido, 83, 102
limitation principle, 10
linguistery, 2, 8
linguistics, 2, 8, 14
Litle Hans, 11, 16–18, 20, 21–2, 69
living, what is [*du vivant*], 41, 48, 96, 102

logic, 40–3, 48, 62–3, 65, 83; mathematical, 41, 91–2; not-all, 77; quantum, 78; of sets, 56–8, 73, 75; sexuation and, 73, 78
L.O.M., 1
loss, 13, 30
love, 13, 28, 31, 98; naming and, 90, 91

man: essence of, 2–3; as name, 1–4
Marx, Karl, 84
masculine universe, 77
master's discourse, 44, 49, 61–2, 81
master signifier, 71–2, 79
mathematical logic, 41, 91–2
mathemes, 25
meaning, 20, 55, 61–2; as signified, 60
Memoirs of my Nervous Illness (Schreber), 82
men: *for-all-man*, 63, 78–80, 85; push-to-woman [*pousse-à-la-femme*], 82. *See also* castration; father; penis; phallus
metaphor, 55; button-tie of language, 7, 12, 57, 70–2, 102; diagnostics according to, 53–4; highway of, 46–8; L and R schemas, 47, 57; paternal, 4, 6–7; words without, 20
metonymy, 8, 15, 28–9, 55
morality, 35–6
motérialité, 16, 20–3, 69
mother, 50, 98; desire of (DM), 49, 51, 53–4; symbolisation of, 11–12, 13
motherland, 76
multiplicity, 78
mystics, 80

name: enigma, 102; father of, 87, 88–9; function of, 89–91; naming and, 95–7
Name-of-the-Father, 44–6, 49–51, 65, 100–1; exception and, 56, 74; plural, 51, 54–6, 92, 93, 95. *See also* father
naming, viii–ix, 46, 54–6, 87; as act, 93, 96, 99; Borromean knot and, 98–101; function of, 91–4; as index, 55–6; man as name, 1–4; name and, 95–7; name changing, 88–9; neurotic and, 93–4; proper names, 89, 91–3, 96; push-to, 92; S, I, R (Symbolic, Real, Imaginary), 92; saying of, 91; symptom and, 97, 103; unnameable, 92–4
nature, sex ratio of, 77, 79
need, 13, 15, 32
negativising effects, 4, 12, 13–14, 32
neurosis, 21, 23, 30, 54, 82; *aphanisis*, 32; as nameless, 93–4

non-relationship, 19, 31, 42, 62, 65, 71
norms, 47–8
not-all, 40–1, 59; of psychosis, 80–3; of society, 84–5; of women, 41, 44, 72, 74, 77–8, 80, 83–4

object: active, 39; child as, 5; women as, 3, 85
object *a*, 5, 8, 13, 23–6, 30. 100; *l'(a)cause première* of desire, 29–30, 34–5; love, metaphor of, 28; in place of semblant, 44
oedipal ideology, 45, 103
Oedipus complex, viii, 4, 100; Antigone and, 28; "beyond Oedipus," viii, 6–7, 45, 56, 63, 88; castration separate from, 62–3; father, function of, 44–8, 50, 52n1, 56, 95; French garden approach, 45–6; good exit from, 50; *historiole* of, 44, 52n1, 56, 101; no discourse of suppléance, 62–3; no longer main attraction, 8, 27–8; normative function, 47–8; three times/consistencies of, 47–8, 50
One, 68, 71, 75, 80, 96
One-saying [*Un-dire*], 59–60
operational reality, 101
order, 35–6, 44, 48–9
Other, 1; analysand as, 37; barred, 25–6, 57; desire of, 14, 65–6; hole of, 5, 12, 58, 92–3, 95; humanisation principle from, 4; jouissance in place of, 82; mirror of, 94; naming and, 90; as nonexistent, 4–7; object *a* and, 25; of the Other, 6, 50, 51, 57; primordial, 51–2; S_1s, 30; speech and, 47–8; as storehouse of signifiers, 53–4; suppléance to, 6
outside-the-universe all [*tout d'hors univers*], 78

paranoia, 54
parent, traumatic, 5–6, 17, 90, 93
parental function, 5, 21, 35
passion, 35
paternal metaphor, 6–7, 25, 469; desire of the mother (DM), 49, 51, 53–4; highway of, 46–8; RUCS and, 7, 10. *See also* father; metaphor
paternal order, 48–51
pathology, 35–6
pédants/pédés, 79, 85–6n3
penis, 84; jouissance, 17, 20, 70; traumatic, 17, 19
perpetuation, 100–1
perversion, 54

phallic phase, 42
phallus, 16–17, 20–2, 24, 49, 65–8; function of, 69–72, 73; jouissance of, 67–8, 69–72, 78–9; not-all of women and, 83–4; psychosis and, 25, 30, 67, 69, 74; as semblant, 78–9; sexed identification, 42, 66; signification and, 49, 55, 65–7, 70–2; without father, 25–6, 69–70, 99–100; without organ, 21
phobia, 15–18, 19–20; as hub, 20–1
Picasso, Pablo, 33
place, 74, 78, 82–3
pleasure principle, 4, 10
political secrets, 64
power, 5, 68, 70
primal repression (PR), 92, 95–6
primordial signifier, 36
propositional function, 73–4
psychiatrist, 81
psychiatry, classical, 54
psychoanalysis: desire, notion of, 23; hatred for, 37; History of, 90–1; language, use of, 2; naming and, 103; object of, 8
psychoanalyst. *See* analyst
psychosis, 3, 21; children and, 10; of great men, 88; not-all of, 80–3; as outside discourse, 54, 78, 80; phallus and, 25, 30, 67, 69, 74

qualifying, 91

racism, 84
Rat Man case, 17, 20
real, 2, 71; hole of, 96–7; logic and, 41; as not One, 96; of subject, 39–40, 100; traumatic, 18
real subject, 39–40
real unconscious (RUCS), ix, 7–8, 15, 19, 71
reason, 77–8
referent, 55; naming and, 88–9, 91
repetition, 5, 6, 68
repression, 4, 30, 55, 92; primal (PR), 92, 95–6
reproduction, 1, 13, 24–5, 44, 88; heterosexuality, 42–3; paternal metaphor, 47–8
Rousseau, Jean-Jacques, 10–11
R.S.I. (Lacan), 15, 17, 19, 20–1, 25–6, 35, 39–40, 65, 74–6; naming, 87, 92, 96, 103
RUCS (real unconscious), ix, 7–8, 10, 15, 19, 71
Russell, Bertrand, 41, 57, 91

S, I, R (Symbolic, Real, Imaginary), 92
S_1, 8, 25, 52, 58, 60, 83, 85
S_2, 8, 25, 44, 52, 58, 60, 83, 85, 102
S(A), 5, 50–1, 58, 93, 96, 100
Sade, 3, 29, 36, 37, 61
saids [*dits*], 16, 41, 49, 59, 61, 65, 73, 92
saint, 90
Sartre, Jean-Paul, 3
Saussure, Ferdinand, 55, 56
saying [*dire*], 38, 56, 73; of analysis, 94; father as, 73, 88–9; function of father and, 41–2, 46, 56, 58–60, 61, 74; God-saying [*dieu-re*], 87–8, 89, 93; half-saying, 87, 92; of naming, 91; One-saying [*Un-dire*], 59–60
Schreber case, 22, 25, 82–4
science, 85
scient, 79, 85–6n3
scoundrels, 37–8
secondary processes, 4, 10
semblant: biological heritage, 79, 84; *thommage* and *dommage,* 78–9
semblants, 6, 10, 28–84, 58, 61, 79, 99–102; family and, 49; interpretation and, 60; object *a* in place of, 44; sites of, 78
sentence, 12
separation, 6
sets, logic of, 56–8, 73, 75
sex ratio, 77, 79
sexual conversion, 103
sexuality, 1, 13; phallus and, 21, 24; reproduction, 24–5
sexual reality, 15–16, 20, 22, 69
sexual relationship, no such thing as, 8, 31, 42, 45–6, 60, 62–4, 63–4, 75–9, 100
sexuation, 24, 31, 55, 88, 91, 100; logic and, 73, 78
signifiable, 55
signification, 29, 49, 55, 65–7
"The signification of the phallus" (Frege), 55
signified, 49, 55, 59–61, 67, 71; desire and, 29–30, 32; name and, 89, 95; production of, 57; unconscious chain and, 27, 30, 60
signifier, 10–11; desire as effect of, 29; emergence of, 52, 53; of exception, 57; father as, 49–50, 75; man and woman as, 78; master, 71–2; phallic, 65–7, 70–2; phobia and, 17–18, 20; primordial, 36; repression of, 95; S_1/R, 20; signified-effect, 55–6, 65
signifying chain, 7, 11, 12, 19, 50; *motérialité,* 20
signifying order, 35, 71–2

Le Sinthome, 19, 40, 45, 68, 69–70, 96, 100, 102
socialisation, 1, 34. *See also* humanisation
social link [*lien social*], 8, 22–3, 27, 48–9, 62–4, 81, 84; naming and, 89–90, 98, 99–100; no discourse of suppléance, 77
social norms, 42
society, not-all of, 84–5
sociology, 45
Socrates, 28
speaking-being [*parlêtre*], 39, 70, 71, 93
species, disappearance of, 42–3
species names, 89
speech, 8, 13, 29, 30; analyst and, 36–7; body of subject, 15; as cause, 69–72; desire and, 62; enunciation, 59, 102; jouissance and function of phallus, 69–72; relation to the Other, 47, 48; satisfaction of, 68; speaking-being, 39, 70, 71
Spinoza, Baruch, 35
Stephen Hero (Joyce), 102
stepladder [*escabeau*], 68, 90, 91
Stoics, 55
structuralist moment, 2–3
structure, 10, 47, 54; as effect of language, 11; of language, 7–8, 41, 54, 59–61, 96, 98
stupidity, 37
subject: denaturing, 11; division of, 25; natural, 13; real, 39–40, 100; S_1/S_2, 7–8; two halves of hetero-sexual couple, 77–9; want-to-be, 12, 24
subject effect, 11
subjective deposition [*destitution subjective*], 39
sublimation, 15, 68
substitution, 20–1
subtraction, 13–14, 24–5, 29–30, 102
superego, 10, 16
suppléances, 6, 46, 56, 78–9, 82; no discourse of, 62–3, 77; oedipal father and, 87
surplus, 2, 33, 38, 44–5
survival of species, 42–3
symbolic, 4, 6, 48, 72, 85; effects on what is living, 11, 14; hole of, 5, 12, 53, 92–3, 95–8; jouissance of, 22; real effects, 11–14; symptom and, 96, 102–3
symbolic chain, 7–8
symbolic order, 7

symbolisation, 11
symptom, 6, 8, 22, 65, 74; childhood and, 15–16; erectile jouissance and, 16–17; father and, 87; hetero-sexuality, 65; identification with, 93, 103; naming and, 97, 103; symbolic and, 96, 102–3. *See also* suppléances

Thing (*das Ding*), 3–4, 12, 51–2, 53, 59, 92, 95
Thomas, Saint, 39
thommage, 78–9
Tiresias, 79
topological place, 75, 78
transcendence, 2
transference, 8, 26
traumatic parent, 5–6, 17, 90, 93
traumatic real, 18, 20
traumatism, infantile, 5–6, 16, 36
trope, 27
truth, 17, 45, 59; castration and, 62; naming and, 88, 92

unarity, 39–40
unconscious, 1; chain, 27; as inhuman, 7–8; jouissance and, 72, 74; knowledge without subject, 19; *motérialité,* 20–3, 1669; RUCS, ix, 7–8, 10, 15, 19, 71; sexual relationship and, 42
Unhappy Identity (Finkielkraut), 6
universal, 73, 77–8, 81
unnameable, 92–4

value judgements, 1
Verhaeghe, Jean-Daniel, 2
victimisation, discourse of, 6
vocation, 35

want-to-be, 12, 13, 24, 30
want-to-enjoy, 13, 24, 30
want-to-know, 13
What Lacan Said about Women (Coler), 67
women: not-all of, 41, 44, 72, 74, 77–8, 80, 83–4; not castratable, 72, 84; as objects, 3, 85; subject proposes to be called, 79–80
work, 20

Y a d'l'Un, 36, 39–40, 64, 72, 100